Learning Through Problems

Learning Through Problems
Number Sense and Computational Strategies
A Resource for Primary Teachers

PAUL R. TRAFTON
&
DIANE THIESSEN

HEINEMANN
PORTSMOUTH, NH

Heinemann
A division of Reed Elsevier Inc.
361 Hanover Street
Portsmouth, NH 03801-3912
http://www.heinemann.com

© 1999 by Paul R. Trafton and Diane Thiessen

The authors and publisher wish to thank those who have given permission to reprint borrowed material:

Cover of *Number Power: A Cooperative Approach to Mathematics and Social Development, Grade 2*, by L. Robertson, S. Regan, M. Freeman, and J. W. Contestable. Copyright © 1993. Reprinted by permission of Developmental Studies Center.

Cover of *Coins, Coupons, and Combinations from Investigations in Number, Data, and Space, Grade 2*, by S. J. Russell, K. Economopoulos, M. Murray, J. Mokros, and A. Goodrow. Copyright © 1997. Reprinted by permission of Dale Seymour Publications.

Cover of *Sorting Groups and Graphs* from *Used Numbers: Real Data in the Classroom* by S. J. Russell and A. Stone. Copyright © 1990. Reprinted by permission of Dale Seymour Publications.

Cover of *Math Trailblazers: A Mathematical Journey Using Science and Language Arts (A TIMS Curriculum)* by the University of Illinois at Chicago.

Copyright © 1997. Reprinted by permission of Kendall/Hunt Publishing Company.

Cover of *Math By All Means: Place Value, Grade 2*, by M. Burns. Copyright © 1994. Reprinted by permission of Marilyn Burns Education Associates.

Cover of *Math and Literature: Book 1 (K–3)* by M. Burns. Copyright © 1992. Reprinted by permission of Marilyn Burns Education Associates.

Cover of *Read Any Good Math Lately? Children's Books for Mathematical Learning, K–6*, by David J. Whitin and Sandra Wilde. Copyright © 1992. Reprinted by permission of Heinemann, A division of Reed Elsevier, Inc.

Cover of *The Wonderful World of Mathematics: A Critically Annotated List of Children's Books in Mathematics* by D. Thiessen, M. Matthias, and J. Smith. Copyright © 1998. Reprinted by permission of National Council of Teachers of Mathematics.

Cover of *Teaching Children Mathematics*, April 1995. Reprinted by permission of National Council of Teachers of Mathematics and the photographer, Jerry Leiberstein.

Library of Congress Cataloging-in-Publication Data
CIP is on file with the Library of Congress.
ISBN 0-325-00126-X

Editor: Hilary Breed Van Dusen
Cover design: Jenny Jensen Greenleaf
Manufacturing: Louise Richardson

Printed in the United States of America on acid-free paper
07 06 05 04   DA   8 9 10

Contents

Preface   *vii*

Section 1: Problem-Centered Learning

Chapter 1	The Pizza Problem Story	1
Chapter 2	A Closer Look	15
Chapter 3	Getting Started: A User's Guide	25

**Section 2: Developing Number Sense
        and Computational Strategies**

Chapter 4	Toward a New Approach: An Evolutionary Process	49
Chapter 5	A Teaching Plan	57
Chapter 6	Children's Computational Strategies	63

Section 3: In the Classroom: Guidelines, Reflections, Ideas

Appendix   *111*
References   *113*

Preface

This book offers a new view of primary grades mathematics; it also celebrates the capabilities and accomplishments of young children. It is based on the work of thoughtful and dedicated primary teachers who have collaborated over several years. They have implemented new approaches and made decisions based on what they believed was right for students. In the process, they have become teacher-researchers who view their classrooms as laboratories. Their students' responses to problems and tasks has been the impetus for them to probe even further into children's thinking. As a result they have made substantial changes in their programs.

The book originates with the work of teachers. In turn, its primary audience is teachers who seek guidance in implementing a contemporary curriculum and instructional approaches. It is subtitled "A Resource for Primary Teachers" because it was written to help teachers learn more about problem-centered learning and provide guidance on how they might implement it. Thus, the book speaks in a conversational voice and addresses the complexities and insecurities of change from a classroom perspective.

The book has two major foci. The scenario of Chapter 1 is problem-centered learning—what it is, what it entails, what we have learned, and how it can be implemented. Chapter 2 describes how number sense and computational strategies can be developed within a problem-centered framework, while Chapter 3 applies the approach to the classroom. The significant finding from the number sense work is that we can have *both* understanding *and* skill—there does not need to be a dichotomy, nor do we need to sacrifice one for the other.

The Background

Our work began seven years ago with the Primary Mathematics Project (PMP), a teacher development effort for first, second, and third grade teachers. The initial goal was to help teachers implement new instructional approaches. It drew upon the pioneering efforts of the Cognitively Guided Instruction Project, the Purdue Problem-Centered Project, teacher collaborative programs, and the work of Marilyn Burns. Our focus became a dual one as we observed the children's strategies and learning. Their work led the project faculty and classroom teachers to explore questions about the implications for the curriculum and children's learning.

The PMP work led us to explore questions about how children acquire number sense and computational strategies under a problem-centered approach. There was strong evidence that children were learning fundamental number concepts and skills in powerful, yet different, ways. This led us to investigate the learning of number concepts and skills in this environment.

A 1995 grant from the Exxon Education Foundation's K–3 Mathematics Specialist Program enabled a group of teachers and University of Northern Iowa faculty to investigate these questions. The first year, the work centered on second grade with the involvement of six teacher-researchers. The second year, we refined and polished the second grade work, while also initiating work with fifteen first grade teachers. During our third year of Exxon funding, the first grade work continued, while second and third grade teachers did initial exploration of children's learning of fraction concepts using a problem-centered approach. The strong Foundation support, together with participation in the Exxon K–3 teacher network, facilitated our work.

Each year, teachers and UNI faculty have gained new knowledge about children's understandings and capabilities. The story has been an evolving one, for each year has brought new insights and findings. And the story continues to unfold.

The Teacher Development Program

From the beginning we sought to establish a collaborative, shared-expertise approach to our work. That is, we believed that both teachers and project leaders possessed special insights and expertise that would contribute to the learning of the other. We felt that through sharing our perspectives and experiences, both groups would grow.

Teachers were encouraged to take ownership of new approaches by implementing ideas in their own ways and on their own schedules. It was accepted that teachers, like the children they teach, learn and change at different rates and in different ways. At the core of our work, however, there was a shared belief about the importance of children's thinking, learning from children, and making curricular and instructional decisions based on our observations. But within this shared framework there was diversity in the implementation of ideas.

In our monthly meetings, summer workshops, and on-line communication much time was devoted to sharing our children's work and our observations, questions, and concerns. Thus, a primary component of our growth was learning from one another as we shared accomplishments and wrestled with issues.

This approach provided an environment that caused teachers to view themselves as teacher/researchers. Often they would select new problems or revisit familiar ones in order to learn more about children's thinking. The excitement of gaining insights from children was a powerful motivator for everyone.

Most significantly, the teachers began to develop a different view of themselves and their work. No longer were they "just teachers;" they believed they were professionals whose ideas were both important and valuable.

The Teacher's Voice

Two of us have served as authors, yet there really have been thirty authors consisting of first and second grade teachers and UNI faculty. In a very real sense, this is the Exxon teachers' book. They have been fully involved at every stage of its development, from reacting to outlines, to critiquing various drafts of the manuscript, to providing classroom examples of children's work, to writing classroom vignettes. They were invited to take ownership of the manuscript and they accepted the challenge of helping shape the story. They have been supportive of the work, but have also served the role of friendly, but firm, critics. This helped us to better understand their work and get the story "right." Needless to say, their input significantly influenced the manuscript.

Thus, in a very real sense this is a book of teachers talking to teachers; that is, a resource by and for teachers. Their voice is always present. Sometimes, it is a direct voice through their vignettes. At all times, it is present in the way the ideas are described.

We invite the reader to join us as we share stories of our classrooms and reflect on the accomplishments of young learners. Their accomplishments should cause us to reconsider what children can do and to rethink mathematics programs and teaching approaches. As you read, celebrate with us the work of our children. We also hope you will be inspired to try these ideas with your students.

University of Northern Iowa Faculty

Larry Leutzinger, *Professor of Mathematics*
Ed Rathmell, *Professor of Mathematics*
Diane Thiessen, *Professor of Mathematics*
Paul Trafton, *Professor of Mathematics*

Project Staff

Mary Friedrich, *Project Coordinator*
Patricia Trafton, *Project Assistant*
Angela Trangsrud, *Project Assistant*

Grade 1 and Grade 2 Exxon Project Teachers

Tammy Bakken, *Lincoln Elementary School, Waterloo*
Peggy Bernard, *Lincoln Elementary School, Cedar Falls*
Laura Bell, *Roosevelt Elementary School, Waterloo*
Sharon Bowling, *Lincoln Elementary School, Cedar Falls*
Lynne Ensworth, *Price Laboratory School, Cedar Falls*
Chris Hartman, *Cedar Heights Elementary School, Cedar Falls*
Linda Hensley, *Dike Elementary School, Dike*
Vi Klosterboer, *Grundy Center Elementary School, Grundy Center*
Melita Meyers, *St. Joseph's Elementary School, Raymond*
Sue Neverman, *St. Joseph's Elementary School, Raymond*
Jan Rowray, *McKinstry Elementary School, Waterloo*
Mary Schneider, *Price Laboratory School, Cedar Falls*
Jill Schulte, *Hansen Elementary School, Cedar Falls*
Bonnie Smith, *Cedar Heights Elementary School, Cedar Falls*
Denise Tallakson, *Price Laboratory School, Cedar Falls*
Cindy Thompson, *Dunkerton Elementary School, Dunkerton*
Dayna Timmerman, *Denver Elementary School, Denver*
Angie Van Wechel, *Dike Elementary School, Dike*
Sharon Walker, *Denver Elementary School, Denver*
Marla Wehrle, *McKinstry Elementary School, Waterloo*
Sue Weinberg, *Dike Elementary School, Dike*
Laurie Wyckoff, *Hansen Elementary School, Cedar Falls*

Section 1

PROBLEM-CENTERED LEARNING

Chapter 1

THE PIZZA PROBLEM STORY

Boys and Girls—We're going to have a pizza party and everyone is going to have 2 slices of pizza. How many slices will we need?

We also need to figure out how many pizzas we need to buy.

The Pizza Shop has large pizzas with 8 slices. How many pizzas do we need to order?

The Pizza Problem[1]

It's mid-September. Already, the second graders are solving problems, sharing their strategies, and working with each other. They are learning to enjoy challenging experiences.

We chose this problem at this time because we felt it

- would challenge the students. They would have to think and reflect on ways to solve it.

- would be accessible. All students would have some way of getting started. Their counting knowledge would enable everyone to be successful.

- would elicit many strategies. This would help all students expand their ways of working on problems.

- was mathematically worthwhile. It would likely expose students to fundamental ideas of addition, subtraction, multiplication, division, mental computation, tens and ones, and multiple ways of counting.

---

[1] This problem also works well with third graders at this time, as well as with first graders int he spring.

But, we questioned, "What would happen when several classes worked on this problem?" Would they find many ways of solving it? Would they take ownership of it and become engaged? Would they work well with other students?

We would soon find out!

Getting Started

A pizza party captures everyone's attention. Students know their teachers believe that they can solve problems. One teacher told her children, "I like giving you these problems because I know you can do them."

Presenting the Problem
Some teachers presented both parts at once. Others had the children work on Part 1 before presenting Part 2.

Working Arrangements
Many children worked in pairs. Teachers know that working collaboratively develops slowly, but are pleased that the children are making progress. Chris reminded her class of some group skills:

- sharing the work
- helping each other
- listening to each other

Using Resources
Children choose their own materials - cubes, markers, calculators, etc. The teacher mentioned where various materials were located and told her students to see if they could solve the problem in two ways.

Letting Go
It's time to let go and see what happens. Children have such original ways of solving problems!

If we want children to become empowered, then they need to take ownership of the problem and its solution.

Working Together

A few moments to get settled . . . and the work begins. The children clearly have taken ownership of the problem.

We are always impressed with:

- how seriously the children take their work,
- how purposeful they are, and
- how well they concentrate.

Even as the children are working—as partners, in small groups, or even independently—we're working as well. We're observing what is happening and asking ourselves important questions.

- How well are they getting started?
- Are they working together well?
- What approaches are they using?
- What thinking strategies are emerging?
- What are individual children doing?
- How might I organize their presentations?
- What strategies need to be highlighted in our seminar?

Sometimes we chat with students to learn more about their reasoning. These conversations help us learn more about each child's thinking and understanding—and this is indeed valuable information for our teaching.

*Caitlin and Robyn thought 26 + 26.
They got out 2 tens but they were
thinking 4 tens. They counted: "Ten,
twenty, thirty, forty, forty-one, forty-
two, . . . fifty-one, fifty-two."*

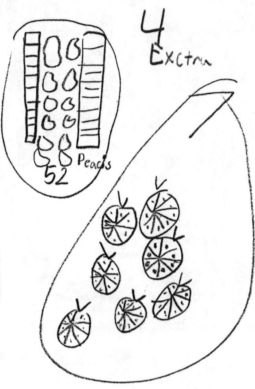

*Damarus wrote 1 through 15 to represent the 15 children. Next he
put 2 dots by each number. Then he counted the dots and got 30.*

Alex and Allison represented the problem using beans.

Greg divided a circle into eight parts. Each time he counted two slices he wrote a number. He rotated the paper as he wrote the numbers around the edge. He drew four circles and noted four pizzas for 15 children with two slices left over.

After making 26 twos with color tiles, Rachel and Ben formed groups of eight to find the number of pizzas needed.

7

The Math Seminar

It's time for the class to come together to discuss their solutions and reflect on each other's thinking strategies.

Children stand before their classmates to present how they solved the problem. As they step forward to share, the rest of the class waits expectantly. Some children bring their written summaries; some bring tools such as manipulatives or a calculator. Some children use the overhead; others use the chalkboard to help explain their thinking.

This is much more than mathematical show-and-tell. It's a powerful time for teaching and learning. Several strategies emerge from the discussion, as many as eight to ten. Some may introduce new mathematical ideas for the children to consider.

We are involved in several ways. We plan the sequence of presentations and make sure that significant new ideas receive attention. We also teach through conducting "mini-lessons," emphasizing new strategies and summarizing the main ideas. Finally, we attempt to involve all children in the seminar.

The clock moves on . . . 30 minutes . . . 40 minutes . . . yet the children are still listening. This is a quiet, serious time—one that they look forward to.

After writing "2" nineteen times, Kristin "chunked" pairs of 2s and wrote "4" below the "4" chunks. To highlight this way of counting, Sue had the class count by fours with Kristin. Sue noted that some children were uncertain.

Sue then had Kristin lead the class in counting by 4s by pointing to the multiples of 4 on the number line. This gave everyone more practice.

To find the number of pizzas needed for 38 slices, one student counted by eights on the hundred chart, while her partner kept track of the eights (or pizzas) using pennies.

Denesha demonstrated how she used the standard paper-and-pencil algorithm, explaining how she had to trade 10 ones for a ten.

$$19 + 19 = 38$$

$$10 + 10 + 10 + 8 = 38$$

$$\begin{array}{r} 1 \\ 19 \\ + 19 \\ \hline 38 \end{array}$$

For 19 +19, Marissa explained, "Take one from a nine and give it to the other nine. That makes ten, ten, ten, and eight." She wrote 10 + 10 + 10 + 8 = 38. Brittany, her partner, drew 19 dots and counted them twice. Both girls were proud of their work.

Analyzing Strategies

One of our primary goals is developing children's mathematical reasoning. Thus, we give careful attention to their thinking - the strategies they use and the mathematical ideas they introduce.

The Pizza Problem led to rich strategies and content, and we learned a lot. Let's see what the children did. For clarity in the following discussion, most examples assume there are 19 children. The discussion is organized around three stages of their work:

- finding the number of slices,
- finding the number of pizzas, and
- dealing with extra slices.

How Many Slices Do We Need?

Interpretation of the Problem

Children interpreted the problem in two ways. Some children thought of it as 19 twos, that is $2 + 2 + 2 + 2 + \ldots$. For them, solving the problem usually involved counting by twos.

The second interpretation involved thinking of the problem as 2 nineteens, that is $19 + 19$. Many of these children seemed intuitively aware that 2 nineteens is the same as 19 twos and chose to use 2 nineteens because it was easier for them to work with than 19 twos would be. Other children reasoned that one slice of pizza for each person would be 19 slices in all. So, two slices for each person would be $19 + 19$ slices in all.

The seminar discussions suggested that the children felt comfortable with both approaches; many of them also made connections between them.

Strategies and Tools

1. Calculators

Some children chose calculators as one of their approaches to the problem. Phil's work led to a discussion about multiplication and the relationship between Charles' and Phil's number sentences. The teacher conducted a minilesson about multiplication, pointing out that 2 x 19 means 2 nineteens or $19 + 19$. Sam added 19 twos, remembering earlier class work that used the contant function. The teacher highlighted Sam's approach by having everyone try this method on their calculators.

- Charles entered $\boxed{19}$ $\boxed{+}$ $\boxed{19}$ $\boxed{=}$

- Phil used $\boxed{2}$ $\boxed{x}$ $\boxed{19}$ $\boxed{=}$

- Sam added $\boxed{2}$ $\boxed{+}$ $\boxed{=}$ $\boxed{=}$ $\boxed{=}$ $\boxed{=}$ $\boxed{...}$

2. Modeling

Some children who interpreted the problem as 19 twos used tiles, cubes, and other manipulatives to represent the problem (see page 7). For those children who interpreted the problem as 2 nineteens, base-ten blocks frequently were used to model their thinking. In some cases, they made two sets of 1 ten and 9 ones; in other cases, they made one set of 1 ten and 9 ones and counted them twice. A few children drew 19 dots and counted them twice.

3. Skip Counting With Symbols

Many children who used skip counting wrote 19 twos and then counted by twos. One child wrote the numbers inside the drawings of pizza slices (see below). Kristin (see page 8) had an interesting variation on this. She grouped pairs of twos to make four and then counted by fours.

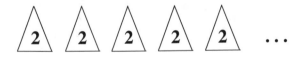

In some cases, instead of writing twos, children wrote the sequence for counting by twos.

$$2 \quad 4 \quad 6 \quad 8 \quad 10 \quad \ldots$$

During one class instruction a teacher asked the children to consider grouping sets of 5 twos to make 10. The ease of counting by tens was also discussed.

4. Invented Strategies

Children used several mental computation strategies, many of which were totally done in their heads. Their thinking is impressive, and it's still September. Here are some of their strategies:

19 + 19

- Add 10 and 10 to get 20.
  Take 1 from 9 and put it with the other 9 to make another 10.
  $10 + 10 + 10 + 8 = 38$.

- 2 tens is 20.
  20 plus 9 is 29.
  29 + 9 is 38.

- Double 10 to get 20.
  Double 9 to get 18.
  20 + 10 + 8 is 38.

- 15 + 15 = 30.
  15 is 4 less than 19, so I need to add 8.
  30 + 8 = 38.

5. Paper and Pencil Computation

The traditional algorithm sometimes occurs, even though it's just September. One student even used the multiplication algorithm. These approaches were discussed, but treated the same as the others. The explanations were thoughtful and meaningful.

```
   1                  1
  19                 19
+ 19               x  2
----               ----
  38                 38
```

How Many Pizzas Do We Need?

Interpretation of the Problem

The Pizza Problem as stated on page 2 consists of two problems. After finding the total number of slices, children must find the number of pizzas to order.

Again, there were two basic approaches. One involved finding the number of eights in 38. In the other approach, children first found that each pizza would serve 4 people and used that information to find the number of pizzas needed.

Strategies and Tools

1. Making Groups of 8

Some children started with 38 counters and made as many groups of 8 as they could. Other began forming groups of 8 until there were 40 counters. Many children made drawings, circling each group of 8. Each circle represented a pizza. Two other approaches are shown on page 7.

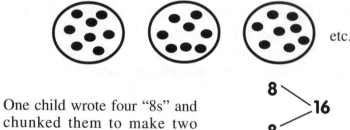

etc.

One child wrote four "8s" and chunked them to make two "16s." He then added 16 and 16. Finally one more eight was added.

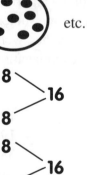

2. Each Pizza Serves 4 People

Many children realized that one pizza served 4 people. It was again fascinating to see the many ways they implemented this approach.

One group, after thinking "four children—one pizza," walked around the room mentally grouping desks by fours. For each group of desks they recorded one pizza.

Another student's work looked like this:

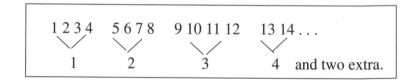

Louis drew five "pizzas" with "4" written next to each one. After adding to get 20, he wrote 20 - 1 = 19 since there were only 19 children in the class.

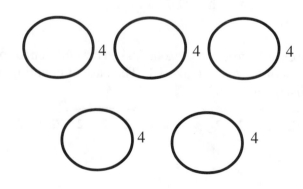

The mathematical ideas of ratio and proportion are generally considered to be middle grades topics and beyond the capabilities of primary grade students. Yet a surprising number of second grade students made use of ratio-like thinking in finding the number of pizzas.

Andy, for example, first realized that 1 pizza would serve 4 people. He used this relationship to (1) determine the number of pizzas that would be needed for 12 people and (2) find the number of people who would be served if there were 6 pizzas. His work shows that he understood that if one doubles the number of pizzas, then the number of people who would get pizza also must be doubled.

> *We want to eat pizza at the end of our school party. There are 24 students and Mrs. Smith in our class. Each pizza has only 8 pieces. How many pizza do we need for each person to get two pieces?*

⊛ 3
4 people
3 pizzas = 12 people
6 pizzas = 24
7. we will have hafe the
pizza

The example at right shows the approach used by children in Anne Smith's classroom. They created a ratio table to "build up" to the number of pizzas needed.

These examples remind us that children are mathematically insightful, and capable of work that is often considered beyond them—*if* we allow them to explore ideas in their own ways. We are again reminded of the power of seminars in exposing all children to the thinking of other children.

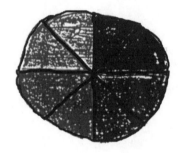

	4 people	=	1 pizza
4 + 4 =	8 people	=	2 pizza
4 + 4 + 4 =	1 2 people	=	3 pizza
4 + 4 + 4 + 4 =	1 6 people	=	4 pizza
4 + 4 + 4 + 4 + 4 =	2 0 people	=	5 pizza
4 + 4 + 4 + 4 + 4 + 4 =	2 4 people	=	6 pizza

Dealing with Remainders

Unless the number of people having pizza is a multiple of 4, there would be pizza left over. In the mathematical realm, this would be beyond the capabilities of second graders. Yet in the context of the pizza slices, children readily understood that one must purchase an extra pizza, even though there would be slices left over. Thus, they readily accepted that they would need 5 pizzas if there were 17, 18, or 19 people.

This situation led to interesting discussions. Some children raised the question of buying a small pizza to take care of the extra 1, 2, or 3 people. One child suggested returning leftover slices for a refund. More typically, children thought of other school personnel who might get the extra pieces, such as the custodian or the principal.

An interesting discussion occured in a class that had 18 people who would eat 36 slices. Some students realized that 4 slices is half a pizza, reasoning that 4 out of 8 pieces is 1/2 of a whole (see diagram). This idea seemed to make sense to students.

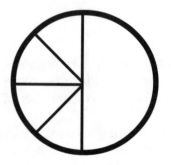

It was particularly interesting to notice how naturally the idea of fractions arose in this applied context. While this situation did not "teach" fractions to the children, it at least planted some seeds that would bear fruit later.

> *"A major goal of mathematics instruction is to help children develop the belief that they have the power to do mathematics and that they have control over their own success or failure."*
>
> *"This autonomy develops as children gain confidence in their ability to reason and justify their thinking. It grows as children learn . . . that mathematics makes sense, is logical, and is enjoyable."*
>
> *Curriculum and Evaluation Standards for School Mathematics* (NCTM 1989, 29)

Section 1

PROBLEM-CENTERED LEARNING

Chapter 2

A CLOSER LOOK

Looking Back

The previous section provided a snapshot of problem-centered teaching and learning. It captured the experiences of six teachers and their children early in the school year. These classrooms

- provided a wide range of strategies,

- enabled us to observe the approach in different settings, and

- helped us learn how different teachers used the approach.

What occurred was exciting. Mathematical reasoning and ideas were discussed, children were actively engaged, and thoughtful discussions occurred.

Yet neither the problem nor the results were unusual. We learned that children have greater capabilities than we realized, enjoy solving challenging problems, and stay engaged for long periods of time. Many problems and tasks produce the thinking and work described.

Key Features

The Pizza Problem illustrates key features of a problem-centered approach. Each teacher has her variations, but generally incorporates the following:

A problem is posed. It may be a "problem of the day" or one that addresses some content or skill. However, all problems need to promote children's mathematical reasoning and their learning.

The teacher briefly discusses resources and working arrangements. We say little about how the children might go about solving the problem. That's up to them.

Children work for an extended period. They choose tools—manipulatives, calculators, markers, newsprint, and so on—and settle down to work. There will be false starts and off-task behavior. But soon they are constructively engaged.

Sometimes we chat with the children about their thinking and encourage them in their work but we avoid intervening any more than necessary.

We make notes as we observe the children. This ongoing assessment is very helpful in our planning. We also identify important ideas to highlight during the seminar.

The work culminates with a math seminar, which has an important role in helping *every* child learn. Children share their thinking with the class and discuss how they solved the problem.

Presenters must clarify and organize their thinking by translating their ideas into words that make sense to others. Reflecting on one's thinking strengthens learning.

As children listen to the ideas and approaches of their classmates, they must think about the problem from several perspectives. They also focus on the language that is used to describe mathematical ideas.

Presentations lead to powerful discussions. We highlight key ideas and look for ways to involve all children. We extend ideas and conduct "minilessons" to develop everyone's understanding.

Mathematical content and processes are introduced and reinforced. Seminars also emphasize that mathematics is a way of thinking, and that justifying conjectures is important. By thinking and working together, children also come to understand that learning mathematics is a collaborative process.

Written records are important. They help children review their work and solidify their thinking. Writing is often recorded in journals and may include diagrams. Writing is often part of the process of solving the problem.

Initially, written work is often fragmentary. However, we enjoy watching the children's improvement throughout the year. Explanations become clearer and more comprehensive.

Rationale and Support

Problem-centered instruction is especially powerful for young children. It enables them to continue learning the same way they acquired a considerable amount of knowledge before entering school—in applied situations.

It lets young children connect their informal, intuitive mathematical knowledge to classroom experiences and to use this knowledge to construct new understandings and skills.

It also allows them to work at their own level and to feel successful regardless of the sophistication of their approach.

A growing body of research and achievement data strongly supports the power of this approach in helping children acquire knowledge and develop the ability to solve complex problems.

A 1995 interview study we conducted found that all children made gains in solving problems and the approaches they used. We were particularly pleased that lower achieving children acquired higher level strategies over the school year. They

"Virtually all young children like mathematics. They do mathematics naturally, discovering patterns and making conjectures based on observation. Natural curiosity is a powerful teacher, especially for mathematics."

"Unfortunately, as children become socialized by school and society, they begin to view mathematics as a rigid system of externally dictated rules governed by standards of accuracy, speed, and memory. Their view of mathematics shifts gradually from enthusiasm to apprehension, from confidence to fear. Eventually, most students leave mathematics under duress, convinced that only geniuses can learn it."

Everybody Counts 1989, 43–44

also substantially narrowed the gap between themselves and the higher achieving children.

Teaching through problems is a central emphasis of reform. The first standard at each level of the *Curriculum and Evaluation Standards for School Mathematics* (NCTM 1989) is "Mathematics as Problem Solving." The first bullet of K–4 Standard 1 states

> *"In Grades K–4, the study of mathematics should emphasize problem solving so that students can:*
>
> *• use problem-solving approaches to investigate and understand mathematical content" (p. 23).*

The first standard of the *Professional Standards for Teaching Mathematics* (NCTM, 1991) is devoted to *worthwhile mathematical tasks*. The importance of having tasks promote reasoning is discussed. While thoughtful activities are still important, the emphasis needs to be on the *thinking,* not just on the *doing.* This is an important shift in our thinking about young children, and creates a different classroom climate and culture.

"Teachers should choose and develop tasks that are likely to promote the development of students' understandings of concepts and procedures that also fosters their ability to solve problems and to reason and communicate mathematically. Good tasks are ones that do not separate mathematical thinking from mathematical concepts or skills, that capture students' curiosity, and that invite them to speculate and to pursue their hunches."

Professional Standards for Teaching Mathematics 1991, 25

About Classroom Environment

Picture yourself in a classroom as the children work on the Pizza Problem. After a few moments of getting settled in a work area, you notice how soon they are intently engaged in their work. For the most part they ignore other children. You overhear bits and pieces of their discussions and find yourself surprised at the quality of their thinking.

Now place yourself at the edge of the group for the math seminar. Again, you notice how deeply the children are engaged in their classmates' presentations and how attentively they sit. When a question is posed, they respond quickly. Some children appear more involved than others, but it is hard to tell by observing. You look at your watch and marvel at their perseverance.

You are participating in the development of a community of math learners. In such a community, children respect and value thinking; they also learn to respect and value multiple ways of thinking and the contributions of others. Children's minds are actively engaged as they think about their work and listen to their classmates. They also act as teachers in the ways they respond to another person's work.

They enjoy solving problems and reasoning mathematically. As they grow as problem solvers, they develop greater confidence in their mathematical capabilities and feel satisfaction from making sense of mathematics for themselves.

Increasingly, children take risks, value mathematical challenges, and work on problems for extended periods of time. They no longer want simple problems—the problems aren't "fun" and they gain little sense of accomplishment. We enjoy observing children's changing images of themselves. They come to believe that they are mathematically powerful and can handle almost any task.

You leave the classroom, but the experience stays with you. You think about the "flow" of the past hour and how focused the children were. You recall examples of children's thinking that amazed and delighted you. You're also aware that the teacher really valued her children's thinking. She listened intently to their explanations and devoted much effort to helping all of her children grow mathematically.

We, as teachers, are also reflecting. We are aware that the children are just beginning their journey in becoming a mathematics community. We know this goal takes a lot of work and time. Yet it is worth the effort because we see progress; in fact, the class seems to be making much quicker progress in the past few days.

About Students

We are delighted by how much we are learning about our students—how they think, what they know, their unique mathematical strengths, and their areas of weakness. We have acquired this knowledge by placing problems and tasks in their hands—letting them view the problems from their perspectives and use their own approaches to solve them—and listening carefully to what they say.

As a result, we have very different views of our students. Instead of focusing on what they *can't* do, we're learning what they *can* do. We're very much aware that in the past we have underestimated their capabilities and are still learning what they *are* capable of doing.

Children's Mathematical Knowledge

Kindergarten and primary grade children possess a great deal of mathematical knowledge—ideas of multiplication, division, fractions, and ratios emerge naturally as they work on problems.

"Students' learning of mathematics is enhanced in a learning environment that is built as a community of people collaborating to make sense of mathematical ideas."

Professional Standards for Teaching Mathematics 1991, 58

They also have resourceful and insightful ways of solving problems. They bring their knowledge and strategies with them to school and share insights with their peers.

Listen to what Primary Mathematics Project (PMP) teachers said about their children:

> *"Children have a lot of informal mathematics in their heads from their everyday experiences."*

> *"Children possess a variety of their own ways of thinking about problems and inventive ways of solving them."*

> *"Children particularly want challenging tasks and problems to work on."*

Think back to the amount of mathematics that emerged from the Pizza Problem— multiplication, division, place value, counting, computational strategies, remainders, and fractions.

The September 1995 interviews with second grade children revealed that students could successfully solve two-step problems as well as ones involving multiplication and division. They also had strategies for computing with two-digit numbers. Their strategies were not always sophisticated, but they understood what to do and how to find a solution.

Children's Growth: Attitudes, confidence, risk taking

Early in the year children are not robust mathematically and lack confidence. It is difficult each year to remember that our new students are not at the same place former students were in May.

But growth occurs—slowly at first, and then faster as the children flourish under the problem solving approach. We notice it in small ways—they work longer before asking for help; math seminars may take less time as children's explanations become clearer.

We've also learned that children value challenge—they soon want problems that make them think and work hard. Many of them even complain if another student gives them the answer.

It is important to note that we observe that *all* children exhibit growth, but at different rates. We each remember the day that Alex, Jessica, or Shawonda made their "breakthroughs" and how good they felt about themselves and the attention they received from their classmates.

Let's listen again to the voices of the PMP teachers:

"Children are confident, expect success, and believe they can solve challenging problems when they are allowed to explore and solve problems their own ways."

"Children stay on task for long periods of time when they work on problems that interest and challenge them."

"Children have positive attitudes, will take risks, and are excited about mathematics when they feel ownership of activities and are able to explore ideas and problems."

Children's Growth: Mathematical knowledge and problem solving capabilities

We have realized that our children learn a great deal of mathematics during the year, including the mainline content that we are expected to teach. Place value knowledge seems stronger than we have ever seen, partially as a result of our ongoing emphasis on mental computation strategies.

Understanding of multiplication and division is strong, and they even try to invent ways of solving problems with large numbers. Fraction work goes far beyond what most second graders learn.

Children's problem solving skills also grow—both in the way they approach problems and in the strategies they use to solve them. However, this growth is not measured by the lesson, unit, week, or even month. It occurs gradually over the year, most of the time in small steps.

Some children start quickly and keep growing. Less mature students cling to immature strategies for a long time. Yet eventually they learn more mature ones. Our more advanced students also grow. Problems can be solved on many levels; these students continue to test the boundaries of their thinking, and enjoy listening to the strategies of their peers and trying them out for themselves. Eventually, some of these strategies become part of their repertoire.

Our primary teachers captured other aspects of their mathematical growth.

The children

- *make connections to other areas.*
- *see mathematics everywhere.*
- *become more flexible in their thinking.*
- *believe there is more than one way to solve a problem.*
- *develop the attitude, "Let's figure it out."*
- *learn from one another.*

From the Classroom

Some reflections . . .

"All the children are discovering concepts or strategies at different times. Some children may be processing what others did two weeks ago. But they are excited and you are excited for them, even though others have experienced it earlier. So, you are always balancing different time frames for each child. You are modifying and designing activities for each child, so s/he can extend in the direction one wants to pursue with the problem."

"You really have to let the children set the pace. Otherwise, I think you would become frustrated and would lose the basis of the program. By letting them set the pace, they will take you where they are ready to go; and wherever they are ready to go, is the place where they are ready to learn. You save so much time by being there at that teaching moment rather than trying to 'pour into their little heads' information that they are just not ready for."

Melita Meyers
St. Joseph's Elementary School

What causes our students to grow so dramatically? Perhaps it is the many opportunities they have to work with content in solving and discussing problems. Perhaps it results from the discussions with their peers and teacher. Perhaps it is their growing belief that they can learn mathematics. Perhaps it is the result of letting children grow at their own pace.

Does change occur? Yes! Does it occur in predictable ways? No! Do we have confidence that all children will grow and change? Yes! Our years of experience have taught us that almost every child will make great strides as junior mathematicians and problem solvers.

About Teachers

Our experiences have caused *us* to grow and change as well—in the way we think about teaching, in the way we plan, in the way we teach, in the way we view children, and in the way we structure the mathematics curriculum.

We brought to our work a longtime commitment to teaching mathematics, a variety of workshop and project experiences, and a knowledge of mathematics reform. But we were still unprepared for how much we would learn as we worked together over the past three years, and for the substantial changes we would make.

Our view of *mathematics* has shifted

from:

mathematics as isolated topics and skills that occur in a logical, well-sequenced, hierarchical order.

toward:

mathematics as connected ideas and as a way of thinking.

Our view of *mathematics teaching* has shifted

from:

telling students what they need to know.

toward:

allowing them to construct their own knowledge.

Naturally, there are times when we need to address prerequisites and focus on skills, and there are times when we need to supply knowledge our children do not possess. Yet our teaching is more and more built around their thinking and their work.

Certainly, we focus more closely on *their* thinking than on *our* teaching, and we modify our teaching based on what we learn from observing and listening to them. Our day-to-day planning is more complex, for what happens one day influences what we do the next day.

The previous section documented what we learned from our students. Building teaching around what we know about our students was a new idea for us. Using this knowledge to guide our teaching has been gradual.

Ongoing assessment is essential to our teaching. We enjoy observing change in our students. We still are concerned about less mature children, but have learned that most of them make far greater gains than with traditional approaches.

We have learned that change is not simple, nor always comfortable. This is particularly the case when it involves letting go of well-established beliefs and practices. Thus change has also been a gradual process—each year we find ourselves moving away from past practices and implementing new ones. Letting go was difficult, but it became easier as we gained confidence in our judgments and decision-making.

The excitement of working *with* our children has been an important influence on our growth. In many ways we feel like researchers working in our "laboratories"—studying children's thinking and learning. This is intellectually engaging, as well as fulfilling!

About Curriculum

Each of our programs unfolds very differently from objective-driven ones, as well as from activity-based ones.

They tend to appear less structured to visitors for several reasons. First, the problems move in a variety of directions and may seem unrelated to each other. Second, one problem often incorporates several mathematical ideas, as we saw with the Pizza Problem. Third, we build on the insights and observations that children introduce. Finally, we realize that some content and processes are learned better when they are developed over an extended period than through a single unit.

Beneath the surface, however, there is structure. We are aware of the major content, skills, and processes that children are expected to learn and we keep careful track of the progress of our students.

We strongly believe that learning does not always occur linearly. Some understandings and skills develop slowly and require multiple exposures. For example, we want children to use such skills as counting on, using a familiar fact to derive a less familiar one, and skip counting. Yet we find that these skills are better developed in the context of multiple discussions over time, rather than in specific lessons devoted to them.

We also find that place value understandings develop as children invent their own procedures for solving problems involving two- and three-digit numbers and as they group objects by tens and ones. We also include miniunits on these topics at various points throughout the year. Materials from curriculum projects have been particularly helpful.

We look for tasks and problems that highlight the main ideas and try to embed individual skills within these broader contexts.

Revisiting major topics during the year and using problems and short units seem to particularly help less mature students.

We have learned that thoughtful ongoing maintenance is a valuable way of helping children master important skills.

We have found it helpful to look beyond individual pieces of knowledge to focus on "big mathematical ideas." A deep, connected understanding of concepts provides anchoring for learning pieces and helps children connect these pieces to each other and to the main ideas.

This approach has led to a richer treatment of content, as children push us beyond standard grade level boundaries. When we think where multiplication, division, and fraction problems have led, we are truly surprised by what children can learn.

The breadth of mathematics that we teach is a second way in which our mathematics programs have changed. As we broadened our view of mathematics, our thinking shifted from arithmetic to mathematics.

As a result, we believe it is important for students to explore and investigate a wide range of mathematical ideas, such as geometry, measurement, data analysis, and patterns. These are natural topics for a problem-centered approach, and we connect this work with our whole instructional program in many ways.

Finally, our programs have changed in the way we use curriculum materials. For example, we no longer depend upon them. We have good collections of resources on which we draw and we learn from each other as we discuss our teaching.

As we noted earlier, we value having access to contemporary materials. Yet we use all materials in flexible ways and make decisions about what portions to use and how to structure the work.

Curriculum thinking and planning is complex, and we still have much to learn. Nonetheless, we feel comfortable where we are in our thinking and look forward to continuing the journey in this area.

Chapter 3

GETTING STARTED: A USER'S GUIDE

Questions Teachers Ask

Planning and Decision-Making

Question 1: How do I get started?

Question 2: Where do I find good problems?

Question 3: Should problems be limited to content children have been taught?

Implementing a Problem-Centered Approach

Question 4: How do I establish a "community of math learners"?

Question 5: Should I provide help when students seem to struggle?

Question 6: What is my role during math seminars?

Issues and Implications

Question 7: What pressures or tensions might I feel?

Question 8: Should I teach specific strategies?

Question 9: Where do manipulatives fit in?

Question 10: Do I still "teach" mathematics?

Question 11: How do I know if my students are *really* learning?

Question 12: How do I connect this work to my basic curriculum?

Questions . . . Questions . . . Questions . . .

Learning new approaches to teaching is difficult. It is even more difficult when these strategies are contrary to past practices and knowledge. We bring to the process our beliefs about how children learn, what their capabilities are, what mathematics content is important, how to sequence the curriculum, and how to teach so that children learn well.

"Adding to" is not nearly as difficult as "letting go." We need to remind ourselves that change takes time, that we change in different ways and at different rates, and that we will have concerns. The Stages of Change Chart at right shows the many steps along the way. We also need to remind ourselves that it's okay to struggle, doubt, and worry.

And, yes, there will be questions—a lot of them initially—and they continue to arise as we test the boundaries of new teaching strategies.

Page 26 lists questions we had as we started. They are also ones that we hear other teachers ask. We hope the discussion is useful as you help children learn mathematics in sense-making environments.

Planning and Decision Making

Question 1: How do I get started?

The First Time: A quick answer to getting started is to "shut the door and pose a problem." That sounds simplistic, but that's what many of us did the first time.

- You're collecting beverage cans and eight children each bring in six empty cans. Aha . . . a "teachable moment": "Class, can you figure out how many cans we collected today?" That's the simple part. It's much harder to stand back and let the children tackle the problem without our guidance.

- You're handing out straws for milk and notice that the box contains 200 straws. You could ask the children how many days a box of straws will last.

Each of us started in a different way—a classroom event that prompted an exploration, a problem that another teacher shared with us, a children's book, or a child's question.

Whatever you do, select a problem or task that allows children to use their own

Stages of Change
Awareness
Familiarization
Experimentation
Routine Use
Integration

Jill Bodner Lester describes the problem she posed to her second graders to begin the school year.

She showed the children a train of 20 cubes. After putting the train behind her back, she broke off 12 cubes and asked the children how many cubes were still behind her back.

This task and related ones were the basis of several days of conversations involving reasoning and problem solving.

Lester 1996, 89–91

16

$8 + 8$ $5 + 5 + 5 + 1$

1 ten and 6 ones $20 - 4$

$2 + 2 + 2 + 2 + 2 + 2 + 2 + 2$

2×8 *an even number*

$100 - 84$

When I'm 16, I can drive a car.

Daily Money Problems

I have 13¢. I want to buy a lottery ticket that costs 10¢. Now if I win the lottery I will get $1.00. I buy the ticket and lucky me, I win the lottery! How much money do I have now?

I have 49¢ in the bank. I went to the store to buy some terminators. Each terminator costs 15¢. How many could I buy? If I get 1¢ a day how many days until I can buy another one?

ways of thinking. This early work gives your students experience with the approach and helps you learn what they are capable of doing. They have much to teach us and they provide the impetus for causing us to go further.

<u>Continuing your efforts:</u> Following a few early experiences, it is helpful to have ideas for problems that will help you grow from *awareness* and *familiarization* into *experimentation*. Many of these ideas will likely be additions to your ongoing program.

Daily routines.   Routines let us experiment on an ongoing basis. For several of us the routines were linked to daily calendar math activities.

• The date or the number of days children have been in school is often recorded. One teacher had her children think of ideas about that number (see Column 1). Over time the variety and complexity of their thinking increased. It is also natural to have children explain their thinking.

• The daily lunch money count is also a part of calendar math. One teacher had students create problems involving the amount of money for each day. This became a very powerful part of her problem solving work over time. She often selected the child a day in advance so he or she could think up a good problem. This routine taught us about

children's interest in solving complex problems and made us aware of the breadth of their knowledge.

• The record of days in school can also be a source of problems. As the number is marked on the number line, many questions can be posed. On Day 34, for example, the children might be asked how many more days until they will have been in school for 50 days.

• Many teachers pose story problems every day. The type of problem can vary and go beyond "joining" and "taking away" ones. The power of this approach is the children's explanations of their thinking. Not only do these problems promote problem solving, they also help children develop a deeper understanding of the operations. Three problems are provided.[1]

Francesca has 18 crayons and Carl has 9 crayons. How many more crayons does Francesca have than Carl?

Drew has 8 marbles. How many more marbles does he need if he wants 15 marbles?

Roberta had 15 pennies. She spent some money for milk. Now she has 9 pennies. How many pennies did she pay for the milk?

---

[1] Page 89 shows several different types of addition and subtraction problems.

Problem solving days. Some problems take only a few minutes to solve and discuss. Others take a whole period or more, such as the Pizza Problem or ones involving a children's book. You might set aside one day every other week for these problems. This provides sufficient time for children to work on the problem and to share their strategies. This also will permit you to explore the problem without feeling rushed.

Replacement units. A number of units have been developed in recent years that build sense-making and problem-centered approaches into the development of major curriculum topics. These units provide the opportunity to experience the power of this approach on a daily basis, and to observe children's understanding and reasoning develop over several days. Some books that we have found particularly useful are shown at the right.

We have presented a few of the many ways that teachers have used to get started. Each of us is different, and you will find the approach that works best for you and your class.

A final suggestion—it is extremely helpful to have a colleague who is also implementing these ideas. This allows you to compare notes, learn from each other, and support each other.

Sample Replacement Units

"Now that I've started, how do I keep it going? Where do I find good problems?"

Good problems—ones that work well with children, stimulate their thinking, and provoke many solution strategies—are all around us. As we learn to give ourselves permission to take risks and trust our judgment, we realize that a prescribed list of problems "that work" is not needed.

However, it is helpful to be aware of resources we can draw upon. Six of these are discussed: children's books, teacher-posed problems, children-posed problems, classroom events, content-based problems, and familiar resources.

Children's Books

In our beginning work, children's books were a major resource. Primary teachers are knowledgeable about reading and language arts, so we felt comfortable with children's books. After all, they set the context for the problem solving.

We were intrigued with the books that we learned about—they were an attractive and imaginative starting point. We knew our children would also find the stories and illustrations interesting.

Additionally, we read engaging vignettes describing a teacher's use of a book, saw examples of children's work, and heard about our colleagues' experiences. The descriptions were like templates, which made the book easy to use and gave us confidence to try other books. We were curious about how *our* children would respond —and we were especially pleased when they went beyond what we had heard and read.

Children's books also provided common ground for meetings in which we shared our experiences and discussed what we were learning. We continue to be delighted to learn about a new book and find new ways of using familiar books.

Each of us has special recollections of our children's work with such books as

> *Ten Black Dots*
> *Rooster's Off to See the World*
> *The Doorbell Rang*
> *17 Kings and 42 Elephants*
> *Math Curse*
> *Counting on Frank*
> *100 Hungry Ants*
> *12 Ways to Get to 11*
> *Pigs Will Be Pigs*

Several excellent resources helped us learn about children's books and offered ideas on their use. Four of these resources are shown on page 31.

Resources on Teaching Children's Literature

Authored by Marilyn Burns, this book describes teachers' classroom experiences with popular children's books. This is the first of a three-book series on using children's literature and is available from several sources.

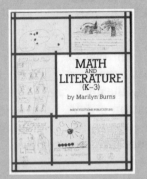

Math and Literature (K–3)

This annotated list of children's books in mathematics contains over 500 entries grouped by topic. Books are rated and recommended age ranges are noted. This bibliography, published by NCTM, was authored by Diane Thiessen, Margaret Matthias, and Jacqueline Smith.

The Wonderful World of Mathematics

David Whitin and Sandra Wilde's narrative describes children's books by topic and provides stories of their use in classrooms. This book is published by Heinemann.

Read Any Good Math Lately?

"Links to Literature" is a periodic department of *Teaching Children Mathematics*, a journal of NCTM. The articles feature classroom teacher's experiences with children's books.

Links to Literature

Teacher-Posed Problems

As suggested previously, we are actively involved in creating and presenting problems gathered from a variety of resources —articles, conferences, workshops, books, and ideas from other teachers.

Some of our problems arise from classroom situations about which we pose a problem. These can be as basic as the number of children who are absent on a day when 18 of 23 children are present, or how many more children ordered hot lunches than brought their lunches.

Some are extensions of a previous problem or a new one that grew out of a previous problem. Each one provides useful information, raises questions, or presents new opportunities.

Some problems are created "on the spot" or occur to us at different times, such as while driving to school. Many times we create a problem because we want to see what the children will bring to it.

Another resource is other teachers. When our colleagues share their students' work we often try the problem with our students to see how they solve it.

The Pizza Problem is a good example of this. One of our teachers created it and later added the question about the number of pizzas to order to make the problem more challenging. When she shared her children's responses, we couldn't wait to try it with our children.

Sharing is just one of the reasons we find it helpful to get together regularly with other teachers or to be connected through e-mail.

We also use problems from familiar resources (see page 29). *A Collection of Math Lessons from Grades 1 through 3* by Marilyn Burns and Bonnie Tank is a helpful resource that provided guidance to us. When we were getting started we modified the "cows and chickens" problem from this book. The children had to find how many feet and tails there are for 5 cows and 4 chickens.

Initially, we were a bit hesitant about posing problems. Over time we learned that most problems work well, and we became more confident in the problems we used. The children are most inventive in how they attack a problem, and the discussions that follow are rich.

Some Interesting Problems We've Used

In basketball you can score 3 points, 2 points, or 1 point when you shoot. The Cougars scored 95 points in one game. How many of each kind of shot might they have made?

A recycling center pays 40¢ per pound for aluminum. Helena weighs 80 pounds. She collected enough aluminum cans to equal her weight. How much money did she get?

A store is selling 4 muffins for $1.20. How much does each muffin cost?

Letticia had 24 valentines. She wanted to share them equally with her friends. How many valentines should she give each one?

Maria scooped out mashed potatoes at a community Thanksgiving dinner. Some people wanted 1 scoop and some wanted 2 scoops. Maria's arm got tired and she stopped after 40 scoops. How many people could she have served?

Nineteen children are taking a minibus to a farm. They can sit either 2 or 3 children to a seat. The bus has 7 seats. How many must sit 3 to a seat, and how many can sit 2 to a seat?

Tyler has saved 30¢. How much more money does he need to save if he needs 45¢ in all?

At noon one day the temperature was 17 degrees. If it dropped 6 degrees each hour, what was the temperature when school let out at 3:30 P.M.?

I have a package of Lifesavers candy. It has 14 Lifesavers in it. How many packages would I need to give everyone a Lifesaver? How many Lifesavers would there be if everyone got a package?

Three children want to share 4 cookies so that each one gets the same amount. How much does each one get?

Suppose that the kings in *17 Kings and 42 Elephants* decided to share the work of caring for the elephants. How could they do this?

The heart stickers cost 15¢ each and the flower stickers cost 10¢ each. Louis spent 60¢ on stickers. What might he have bought?

Children-Posed Problems

We quickly learned when we were getting started that children have wonderful ways to solve problems. It took a while longer and some additional "letting go" before we realized that they are a source of creative, interesting, and challenging problems. This was one more thing they taught us.

Their problems come from many sources. Sometimes a children's book is the stimulus. *Alexander Who Used to Be Rich Last Sunday* served this purpose in one classroom. The teacher challenged her children to create problems in the spirit of the book. And they did—with the same quirkiness and humor as the book. In another classroom, children created problems about the animals illustrated in *17 Kings and 42 Elephants*.

Math Curse and *Counting on Frank* also led to interesting problems. We were surprised that second graders could pose challenging problems that capture the flavor of the books.

As noted earlier, in some classrooms children created problems for the number of the day. As the year progressed, their problems became increasingly complex.

In January, one student stated that the computation in the problems was much too easy—he wanted harder ones. The teacher inquired, "Well, what would be a harder problem?" The child paused and then said, "Well, figuring out how many hours there are in a week would be a good one."

The teacher wondered whether children would be able to deal with 7 twenty-fours. But trusting children's capabilities means trusting them to find ways of solving "messy" problems. So, she let them work—and they succeeded. Each pair had an appropriate approach and almost every pair had the correct answer. Two days were devoted to this problem—a day spent on solving the problem and a day spent on sharing their seven different strategies. It was time well spent.

Children have much they want us to understand about what they know. These interactions not only help us understand that they are wonderful problem solvers, but they also helped us understand that they are wonderful problem posers. Our classes are much more exciting as a result. They are delighted to be sharing the responsibility of posing problems and we are no longer the sole source of problems.

Their problems also help us with evaluation. By noting the difficulty level of the problems they posed, we are better able to plan instruction that matches their backgrounds.

Kids Write Great Problems

Math Curse Problems

We're having ice cream for dinner. A carton of ice cream only serves 4 people. We have 6 people in our family. But my grandparents and 2 cousins are coming, too. How many cartons of ice cream do I need? How many more people can we invite?

Light bulbs come in packages of 2. We are building a new house. We need 100 light bulbs. How many packages of light bulbs do we need?

Mrs. F. is going to the gym. And they have 24 kids in their class. Then 6 more classes come in. And they each have 24 kids. But one class from 6th grade has 10 kids. How many kids now?

There are 23 kids. 7 girls and 16 boys. The 7 girls wore gloves. The 16 boys wore mittens. Half the boys lost one mitten each. How many gloves and mittens are there on the kids' hands?

How Many Feet in the Bed?

Mom and Dad were in the bed and one cat jumped in, too. Next came the dog, two twins, Aunt Jane, and Aunt Betty, and Herman the caterpillar who had six feet. How many feet in all?

We had 150 cookies and we had 6 friends over. Friends came over and they all took some cookies until they each got the same amount. How many did they each get?

I went to the Renaissance Festival in Shakopee, Minnesota where I went fencing. Each time I fenced it cost 17¢. If I had 53¢ to spend, how many times could I go?

Yesterday there were 26 hours and today there are 26 hours and tomorrow there are 26 hours. How many hours in all?

(Note: The child knew there are 24 hours in a day, but chose 26 because he had a new strategy in mind.)

Counting on Frank Problems

Frank went to the store to buy jelly beans. Each jar had 100 jelly beans in it. Frank eats 20 jelly beans every day. How many days does it take Frank to eat all of the jelly beans?

Frank eats three bones in one day. The bones cost 90¢ each. How much does it cost to feed Frank for two weeks?

My mom and dad say, "You have a brain, use it!" So I do. My dog Frank is pretty big. Frank can drink 5 gallons of water a day. Each gallon costs $2.00. How much money would they have to spend to feed Frank water for one week?

There are 25 cookies lying out in the road. The cookies were in a jar in this one town. No one lived in this town except ghosts. There were 10 ghosts in this town. How many cookies did each one get?

Charlotte's Web Solutions

Julie's Solution:

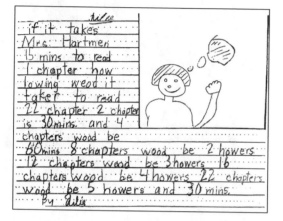

John's Solution:

Classroom Events

Classroom Events

On Monday in Math Class, Mrs. Fibonacci says, "You know, you can think of almost everything as a math problem."

This opening quote from *Math Curse* captures what frequently happens when children believe that they are powerful problem solvers and that mathematics is everywhere. As a situation arises or a question is posed, a math problem emerges just waiting to be solved.

- A teacher was reading *Charlotte's Web* to her class when a child asked if the movie version contained everything that was in the book. Some children said that the movie couldn't because it would be much too long.

Someone asked how long it would take to read the book. So they timed how long it took to read one chapter. They inquired about the number of chapters. "Let's see . . . 15 minutes . . . 22 chapters" and the problem was pursued in the midst of the reading period (see Column 1).

- In another classroom, second graders were studying "Staying Healthy." The topic of germs came up, and someone asked how fast germs multiply. They double every 20 minutes.

The children were quickly into a math exploration. Starting with one germ, they first found how many there would be in 1 hour, and then they decided to double until they got to 3 hours. Most of them continued to work with partners, extending the problem to 5 hours . . . and some went far beyond 5 hours. It was an unexpected adventure in the middle of health class.

Young children haven't learned to put boundaries around their thinking or their learning. Once they acquire the belief that they are supposed to be thinkers and problem solvers, problem solving is no longer limited to "math time." In their minds, math time is all the time.

What makes this kind of problem solving so special is that it is *truly* problem solving with a purpose—there's an immediate reason for solving the problem, and thus the problem solving is *authentic*.

At first we had to work at giving ourselves permission to let go of what we were "supposed to be doing," in order to work on a problem. Over time we knew problem-centered learning fits a larger, more comprehensive agenda.

Content-Based Problems

The systemic development of mathematics such as place value, fractions, probability, and multiplication traditionally occurs in a linear progression from basic to more advanced tasks—but there is another way.

Content can also be developed through carefully selected problems and tasks. These can launch new topics and provide insights to teachers about the knowledge their children already possess.

As we learned more about the content we teach, we developed a greater understanding of the key ideas and built connections among them. Focusing on these ideas helps children understand the content and provides anchoring for the "pieces."

• The idea of grouping underlies place value. To develop children's understanding of describing "how many" in terms of the number of groups and leftovers, we created an activity. Each child takes a handful of buttons. They group them by 2s, 5s, or 10s and report the total in terms of how many groups and how many ones leftover.

The next day the children decided in which interval (25–29, 30–34, 35–39, etc.) their number of buttons belonged, and made a graph from these results.

We wanted the activity to promote learning about groups and leftovers—and to highlight the mathematics. The mathematics often gets lost if the emphasis is on *doing the activity* rather than *doing mathematics*. Three examples of activities that promote learning about fractions follow.

• A teacher had her children make a pattern block design in order to engage them in a discussion of how lines of symmetry divide a figure into halves. She planned to focus on the idea of "halveness."

• Another teacher chose sharing 3 cookies among 4 children—and had paper circles available. She knew this would lead to a discussion about equal-size pieces and fraction names. It would also provide insight in what students knew about fractions from their everyday experiences.

• A third productive task involves making 4 equal-sized regions on a geoboard. There are many solutions, including ones in which the 4 parts have the same area, but are not congruent. The discussion about whether these pieces are "fourths" is always interesting. One of the things we also like about this task is that it leads naturally to eighths—an even more interesting task to explore.

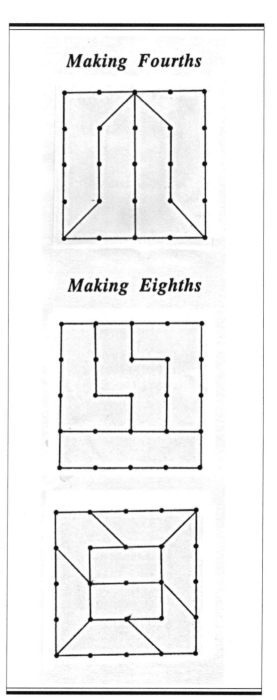

Making Fourths

Making Eighths

Familiar Resources

Every teacher has a collection of resources gathered over the years—activity books, supplemental textbook material, teacher's guides, handouts from workshops, back issues of journals, and so on.

Many of these materials are no longer a direct fit with our present focus on reasoning and learning through problems. But in our busy lives, there isn't time to find all-new resources. Yet we do find familiar resources are still useful to us. While they are no longer the primary source of our ideas, they are part of our planning.

Many times we look at a familiar idea and find a way of recasting an activity or problem to fit our present work. This process reminds us that *we* make the key decisions about our teaching. Even when the idea doesn't quite fit, we find that it has started our thinking in a productive way.

There are so many good sources for problems. The way these sources "work together" to help us challenge our students and develop their mathematical reasoning and understanding is exciting. The more of this we do, the more possibilities we see.

Question 3: Should problems be limited to content children have been taught?

Traditionally, it seemed natural to place limits or "boundaries" on problems. Early in the year, we just used addition and subtraction problems, and we emphasized one-step problems before including two-step ones.

But what seems logical doesn't always fit what children are able to do. Children grow up in a world that is full of problems. For five years they have solved many complex problems to attain their goals—playing a game with peers or parents, finding channel 24 on the TV, puzzling out how much two 15¢ items would cost, etc.

Drawings, manipulatives, and counting strategies are powerful techniques that serve children well in solving problems. Their knowledge of various ways of thinking about numbers often enables them to deal with the computation in novel ways. While we may view a problem as involving subtraction or multiplication, this is not necessarily how the children view it.

Their life experiences are also a powerful resource. A child who has several brothers and sisters may never have heard of division or fractions, but may be quite skillful in solving "sharing situations."

We also note that children are working on these problems with partners, so the knowledge that is needed to solve a problem is distributed among several children. Also, sharing in math seminars is a learning time for many.

Further, the purpose of these problems is not only the solution, but the thinking processes used. Our work is a tool for promoting mathematical reasoning, for "planting seeds" to be nurtured at some point, for assessing children's knowledge, and for learning what insights they already possess.

It's sometimes difficult to realize that things we now take for granted were once issues for us. So much of what we have learned has been taught to us by our students. They are patient and gentle, yet persistent, teachers.

There are times when we may still wonder if a problem or task is within the children's capabilities. Sometimes we may even slightly simplify it. But most of the time they do extremely well, and we wonder why we worried.

Question 4: How do I establish a "community of math learners"?

Establishing a community of learners— that is, developing a group climate that supports thinking and sharing thinking, values the ideas of others, and encourages risk taking and learning from others—is the primary agenda each fall. We know that establishing our mathematical community will take time—sometimes a few weeks and sometimes two or three months; we also know that it will occur.

We work hard at building this community and each fall we have to remind ourselves of the complexity of this task. Each of us has had classes that moved fairly quickly in becoming a mathematical community and each of us has had classes that had much greater difficulty and took more time.

The dynamics of orchestrating this has been powerfully captured by Jill Bodner Lester in "Establishing a Community of Mathematics Learners." Some thoughts from the introduction to her article are cited in the column at right.

There is no one approach that works "best." We know we want to establish a reflective environment, to encourage

---

Establishing a Community of Mathematics Learners

"It's exciting. It's frightening. It's September and time for a new beginning. . . . I spend weeks picturing what I would like math class to be . . . I want to set a tone. I want the children to know that mathematics involves thinking and the development of problem-solving strategies.

I want them to feel safe and to feel that they can risk asking a question or sharing an incomplete idea. I want them to listen to one another respectfully and to try to understand what their classmates are thinking and doing. I want them to learn to formulate their own mathematical questions and to take responsibility for their own learning. . . .

I have learned that the skills I'd like the children to acquire develop slowly. Within the context of solving mathematics programs, the children gradually become more confident and more comfortable, and over time they learn that this classroom is a safe place to pose questions and to pursue answers. It is an environment in which curiosity, questioning, and exploration are respected and encouraged."

Lester 1996, 244

children to think and be involved in sharing their thinking with others, and to participate in math seminars.

We begin with these goals and slowly work toward them. We remind children about what will be valued in our classrooms, and we create familiar routines so that they are reminded daily of our approach to mathematics. We also try to be consistent in our approach from day to day, and to provide sufficient time for them to reflect and share.

Slowly, children begin to understand and value our efforts. A major impetus for community building is the power and satisfaction that children experience under a problem-centered approach. It "feels good" when children know they have solved a problem through hard work; it "feels good" when they learn a new strategy; and it "feels good" when their peers value their thinking.

Still, it is hard work and we remind ourselves at the beginning of each school year about the patience, time, and effort that will be required. However, when the community begins to develop and we see the power of our children's thinking, we reaffirm that it was worth the effort.

This was a real dilemma for us. Teachers are typically expected to give explicit directions and step-by-step guidance to ensure that children don't have difficulty. We remember being taught to model what the children are to do. This has led to the widespread tendency to "keep things simple" for young children and "set them up for success" rather than to "set them up for thinking."

Thus, our initial response when we see children starting slowly, seeming to struggle, or moving in wrong directions is to rush in and "rescue" them. We have since learned that dilemmas and struggles are an important part of learning and are necessary to helping children grow mathematically. The children come to expect problems to be challenging and to take time; in fact, they are disappointed when problems don't cause them to think hard.

We talk with children about their work, often asking them to explain what they are thinking—both when it is correct and when it is incorrect. Sometimes, this helps clarify misconceptions.

If a child is genuinely confused, we may suggest using smaller numbers. On occasion, when we sense that many children do not understand a problem, we have held a brief discussion with the whole class about their thinking.

Yet we try not to give "hints" that essentially tell the children what to do. We are uncomfortable about helping them get "back on track" through direct intervention, as we may be imposing our thinking and structure on children rather than helping them construct their own.

Children often come to the math seminar with incorrect solutions. After listening to the solutions of others, they may ask to continue their work on the problem. We recall when children have wanted to share mistakes; after presenting their solutions, they explain their errors. The children also have become very supportive of one another and understand that errors are a natural part of doing mathematics. Errors often can lead to new understandings about the concept.

Dilemmas don't have simple answers. We do what we think is best at the time and reflect on the decision later. We have become more comfortable about dealing with complex decisions and more confident about making them. Conversations with other teachers have also helped us.

Question 6: What is my role during math seminars?

Seminar time is when children share their thinking and strategies—but it is much more than this. It is a time when all children become aware of alternative strategies and new concepts. The children who present must translate their thoughts into words that communicate to others. As children organize and clarify their thoughts, their learning is strengthened.

It is powerful for children to hear the thinking of others. During seminars, they become aware of multiple ways of thinking about a situation. Various solutions, expressed in the children's own words, often connect with a child who is struggling.

During the seminar, a great deal of mathematics is learned—both content and ways of reasoning. The discussions highlight that *mathematics is a way of thinking* that involves justifying one's conjectures and that *it is a collaborative process.*

High-quality seminars do not happen overnight; it takes time for primary children to learn how to present, to share, to think—but they do learn how. We have an active, essential role in making seminar a powerful and productive time.

From the Classroom

"One powerful aspect of seminars is the way students learn to respect the mathematical ideas of others. They say, "You added 10 instead of subtracting 10," rather than, "That is the wrong answer." All children participate at their own levels. Less mature students are actively sharing their strategies that are based on counting or manipulatives. Their contributions are as celebrated as those of the most advanced children.

Reflecting on reasoning and processes enables all children to make sense of mathematics for themselves. And it is truly a cooperative learning environment, not a competitive one."

Sue Weinberg
Dike Elementary School

Our planning for seminars begins during the work period when we gather information by observing the children's work and talking with them. We note approaches to highlight and consider ways of organizing the presentations.

It is important to create an atmosphere in which thinking about their thinking is valued. When gathering for the seminar we make sure that the children are prepared to listen. If they are gathered on the rug in front of us, we remind them to sit "at attention" because other children are their teachers. But we have learned that even a restless child may be learning more than we initially thought.

When everyone is ready, we have a child describe his or her work and make sure that everyone heard the explanation. If a new strategy occurs, we need to highlight it and perhaps conduct an "on-the-spot" minilesson. Learning strategies in context are particularly powerful for children.

To maximize learning, we often

- ask a child to restate what was said,
- ask if others thought the same way,
- have them verbalize the strategy to a partner,
- engage the class in trying the child's strategy,
- create another example to which the child's strategy can be applied,
- ask children if they can remember other problems this strategy was used for,
- give key strategies a name and build our own class list, or
- summarize the strategies that have been presented.

We found it takes time and practice to make this a highly productive part of our teaching. The more we learned to listen to children and to build on *their* thinking, the more valuable seminar time became.

Question 7: What tensions or pressures might I feel?

We have noted that change is complex—not just because it involves new goals and strategies, but because it also means dealing with old beliefs and ways of teaching. It means going against the entrenched culture of mathematics teaching.

As we grow to value mathematical sense-making as a central focus of our teaching, we face several issues, including

- letting go of past beliefs and practices which may have served us well,

- being willing to take risks, and

- learning to trust our judgment and insight in making decisions about our teaching and children's learning.

It may help to examine the behavioral aspects of the instructional approach that many of us once used:

- single-objective lessons,
- incremental (step-by-step) learning,
- limited concept development,
- skill emphasis,
- reliance on routine practice, and
- teacher as primary source of knowledge.

A behavioral approach has clear expectations for the work of teachers and children. It also has shaped the expectations of parents, fellow teachers, and administrators.

For us, the old way was familiar, predictable, and "safe." However, not only is there little research supporting this approach, but there is also ample evidence of its failure in helping students learn and think.

There is, however, consistent and comprehensive research over sixty years that emphasizes that developing understanding and relationships, together with building on children's thinking, promotes learning. Cognitive research on problem-centered learning has added to this base.

Most of us also had experience with activity-based approaches. We believe that manipulatives are important and we value good activities; however, we now focus more on children's mental activity. We also have higher expectations of children's capabilities.

Change for us involved reexamining our past teaching, as well as traditional norms and expectations. On the other hand, the new approaches helped us address past concerns about student learning; this wasn't simply another trend, but a progression to using more of what we know about teaching and learning.

We were aware that we were taking a risk by choosing to teach in less predictable and secure ways. The risks included questions and concerns of administrators, fellow teachers, and parents. Several factors emerged that helped us deal with these concerns.

A major factor in moving forward has been the children; we appreciated their enthusiastic responses and gained a new appreciation for their capabilities. We observed them becoming more mathematically competent and confident. They also were learning more and better mathematics. At times, we think this is partially a matter of simply letting them show us what they already knew.

A second factor was our growing knowledge of research and professional literature. This literature gives us greater confidence in our teaching and suggests how to increase our effectiveness.

Another factor has been our process for change. We kept things manageable so that we remained in control of our teaching.

We began slowly and abandoned reliance on our textbooks only when we were ready, although we had begun the process of "pulling away" from them months earlier. At times we used conventional worksheets and tests to assure ourselves that our students were learning the content we were expected to teach.

A fourth factor has been the response of the parents. Although we worried about their reactions, it has been a pleasant surprise to learn how pleased most of them are. After all, their children come home and share examples of the wonderful and powerful things that are happening. We keep them informed, letting them know, for example, what we are doing with basic facts and other traditional skills. At times we assign exercises of various types for homework. If parents express concern, we explain what we are doing, show them samples of their child's work, and invite them to visit the class.

We have not chosen the simplest or safest path for our mathematics teaching. There are still days when we have concerns, but we realize this is natural.

We can't go back because our children are learning so much more and we are enjoying what we continually learn about them. We think of where we have come in the past five years and choose to keep moving forward. And best of all, each day holds the potential for wonderful insights and new learning.

Question 8: Should I teach specific strategies?

Children's problem solving and computational strategies are the primary focus of our classrooms. We want children to learn a wide variety of strategies and we work hard to ensure that all children learn them. Yet we do very little direct teaching of them, in the sense of devoting lessons to specific strategies or teaching specific strategies for particular problems. (Computational strategies are discussed in Chapter 2.)

We are aware of the research on children acquiring mature and appropriate ways of thinking. Strategies are not learned at a specific time or in a single lesson. Children will use them when they are ready.

We structure situations to promote their use, but realize that the child has to decide to use them.

Being able to use strategies is important for all of our students, including the less mature ones. It takes effort and time, but most children gradually acquire them. Again, it is on their timetable, not ours.

Our experience shows that children naturally and successfully find their own ways of solving a problem, and then engage in reflection about the approaches they used. Many strategies emerge this way; our job is to highlight them and ensure that children understand them. Children are curious about new ways of thinking and often attempt to use them on their own.

Question 9: Where do manipulatives fit in?

We are well aware of the important role of manipulatives in learning mathematics. They help children develop and clarify concepts.

Yet in one area of the use of manipulatives we struggled. We found that with smaller whole numbers many children relied on manipulatives to find answers by count-

ing. That is, after children modeled a problem, they would simply count.

Our concern was that manipulatives perpetuated counting among children who were capable of learning more mature strategies, such as counting on, derived facts, or reasoning with tens and ones. This led to many questions and concerns about the role and use of manipulatives.

Our concerns caused us to reflect on the positive and important roles manipulatives *do* have in learning mathematics. In the area of problem solving, one important role is in representing or modeling a problem. Consider this problem:

> 23 children are going on a field trip.
> 3 children are going to ride in each car.
> How many cars are needed?

Taking 23 cubes and making groups of three is very helpful in understanding the action or structure of the problem. (This also could be accomplished by drawing a picture or having children act it out.)

A second role of manipulatives in solving problems is providing verification of one's reasoning. For example, a student might solve a problem involving 48 + 23 by mentally reasoning, *"40 and 20 is 60, 60 and 8 is 68, and 68 and 3 is 71."*

When the child verifies her thinking using base-ten blocks, it helps her clarify her ideas. This also makes it easier to explain her thinking to the class. As a result, all children have a chance to understand the strategy. The discussion also strengthens children's understanding of place value.

We also encourage children to use more than one method of solving a problem; as a result, a child who "counted all" might use reasoning with numbers as a second approach. We remind ourselves that class discussions also contribute to making children aware of many possible approaches.

Reflecting on this question has been beneficial. We've clarified our thinking and reinforced *when* and *how* we use manipulatives.

> **Question 10: Do I still "teach" mathematics?**

Yes! Each of us still *teaches* mathematics. Often we do it differently than we did before, but there are also times when we present information, introduce terminology, identify the components of a skill, introduce connections among mathematical ideas, or ask questions that cause children to extend their thinking.

Teaching is often discussed as "dispensing knowledge" or "facilitating learning," as if these were distinct entities, rather than points along a continuum. We must be careful of creating artificial dichotomies. We must also be careful not to think of being a "facilitator of learning" as a passive role for a teacher.

We consider ourselves facilitators, for we do share ownership of tasks and knowledge with our students, and they help us shape lessons and discussions. Yet we are very active teachers, whether we are talking with students, directing a math seminar, or selecting rich tasks to promote new learning.

The more we learn about teaching through problems, the more mathematics we are able to develop in this manner, particularly as we become more knowledgeable about the main content ideas. However, this knowledge grows slowly and skill in "pulling things together" at appropriate moments develops gradually.

The answer is "yes." We still teach in both old and new ways. But the main goal is always that our students make sense of mathematics.

Moving away from established approaches carries risks (see Question 7). Because our teaching is not tied to highly specific objectives and we view learning as occurring over an extended period of time, we don't have the same sense about whether our students are "really learning." Actually, this was a false sense of security, for we remember going over the same content again and again.

However, we don't have a lot of "smiling faces" on worksheets to acknowledge completed work. We actually have more evidence—and in different forms—than we did traditionally. We note important aspects of and changes in children's thinking. We often carry a clipboard on which to record our observations. On reflection, we know so much more about our children's performance and understanding than we ever did before.

We have accepted that meaningful assessment involves samples of children's work, notes from classwork or seminars, conversations with a student, and their "mathematical dispositions" (see column at right). We have learned that assessment is ongoing and we need to listen to their explanations to gauge their knowledge.

Transitions to new ways of assessing have taken time. Although we recognize that our knowledge of each child's thinking is important, we initially had three concerns.

First, we worried about how parents would react to our new approach to assessment. Actually, parents are pleased that we can tell them so much more about their child's performance and feel that they learn more from their child's work by our observations.

Second, we were concerned about how students would do on achievement measures, such as criterion-referenced and standardized tests, which often focus heavily on traditional skills. We knew they were learning . . . but would their knowledge be measured on tests that have traditionally been valued? The performance of our children, as well as those from similar projects, shows that they are learning basic concepts and skills at a high level. Additionally, they demonstrate mathematical knowledge and problem solving capabilities beyond traditional expectations for primary children.

Third, it is true that children learn at different rates. We learned that these differences are easier to accommodate in a problem-centered classroom than in a traditional one. Children achieved by having opportunities and time to learn a concept or strategy.

NCTM Evaluation Standards

Standard 10: Mathematical Disposition

"The assessment of students' mathematical disposition should seek information about their

- *confidence in using mathematics to solve problems, to communicate ideas, and to reason;*

- *flexibility in exploring mathematical ideas and trying alternative methods in solving problems;*

- *willingness to persevere in mathematical tasks;*

- *interest, curiosity, and inventivenesss in doing mathematics;*

- *inclination to monitor and reflect on their thinking and performance;*

- *valuing of the application of mathematics to situations arising in other disciplines and everyday experiences;*

- *appreciation of the role of mathematics in our culture and its value as a tool and as a language."*

NCTM 1989, 233

Question 12: How do I connect this work to my basic curriculum?

As noted earlier, we moved gradually in changing our curriculum. This gave us time to feel comfortable with new approaches and ensured that our students were still meeting our districts' expectations.

We gradually moved from two programs—one that occurred during "morning math" time, for example, and one that we considered our standard one—to a more unified one. This beginning is similar to teachers who originally designated one day a week as problem solving day. They soon realized that problem solving is not a separate strand.

The typical primary grade curriculum is not very ambitious and includes extensive review and much attention to traditional computation. As we began to make computation an ongoing focus, we found that we had sufficient time to move in new directions. Some of this time was devoted to interesting and challenging problems that addressed other curriculum topics. Some of this time involved the use of contemporary units that incorporated a problem solving approach.

Over time we have moved to organizing our program around the key ideas we feel are important. Often, these ideas unfold through problems, supplemented by blocks of time that pull the ideas together. Our teaching of money, for example, has shifted from a "unit" to an ongoing emphasis supplemented with short periods of direct focus.

Content areas such as data analysis and measurement naturally lend themselves to a problem solving approach. A data collection project, for example, incorporates high-level decision-making throughout. We're also discovering that such traditional topics as fractions, multiplication, and division occur naturally throughout the year with children achieving high levels of understanding of them.

We found that it is initially important to focus on feeling comfortable in handling the key elements of a sense-making approach for one or two topics. Gradually, more topics were included as we gained experience and confidence.

At times, our ongoing curriculum planning seems complex, but it is manageable. We become increasingly comfortable in a more fluid, yet focused, approach to our mathematics programs.

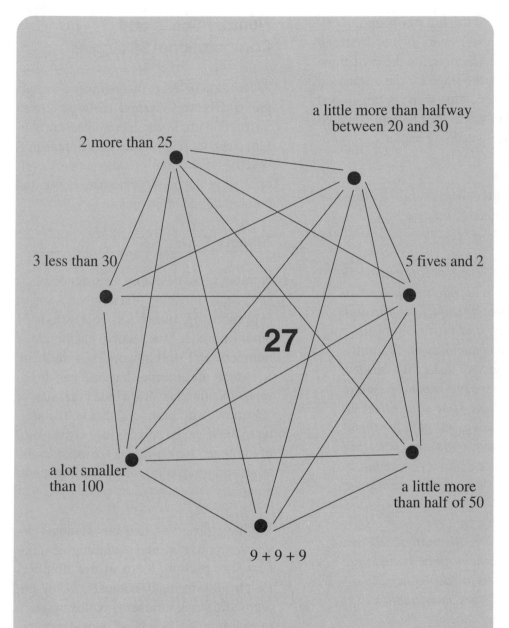

a little more than halfway
between 20 and 30

2 more than 25

3 less than 30

5 fives and 2

27

a lot smaller
than 100

a little more
than half of 50

9 + 9 + 9

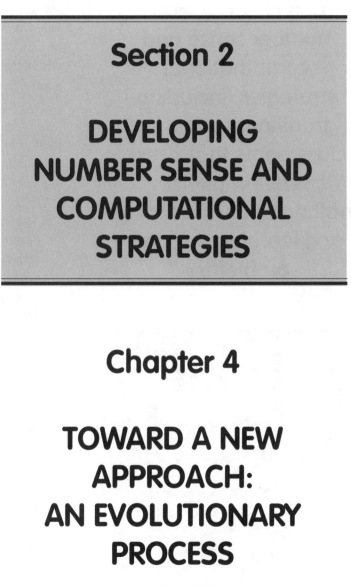

Section 2

DEVELOPING NUMBER SENSE AND COMPUTATIONAL STRATEGIES

Chapter 4

TOWARD A NEW APPROACH: AN EVOLUTIONARY PROCESS

Can children learn number sense and computational strategies, including traditional skills, in classrooms that stress sense-making, mathematical reasoning and learning through problems?

> *"Number sense can be described as good intuition about numbers and their relationships. It develops gradually as a result of exploring numbers, visualizing them in a variety of contexts, and relating them in ways that are not limited by traditional algorithms. . . . (Textbooks) cannot replace the 'doing of mathematics' that is essential for the development of number sense."*
>
> Howden 1989, 11

The question at the left has been the primary focus of the work of our first and second grade teachers for the past three years and sets the stage for the discussion of this chapter. Our work is positioned within the context of the problem-centered approach presented in Chapter 1.

First, a brief recollection of the effects of a problem-centered approach:

> *Students learn mathematics in classrooms in which mathematical sense-making, learning through problems, and participating in a learning community occurs daily. They approach tasks with the view that there is a problem to be solved. They devote time and effort to thinking things through for themselves and consider multiple approaches. They become mathematically capable and confident.*

> *"Knowing mathematics" means using mathematical knowledge and insights to "do mathematics." They also view mathematics as a unified and cohesive whole.*

Number Sense and Computational Strategies

A common belief is that number concepts and skills are learned through direct instruction in a linear, hierarchical curriculum. Our work provides a different perspective of children's mathematical development in the areas of number sense and computational strategies.

Number Sense

Number sense describes a cluster of ideas, such as the meaning of a number, ways of representing numbers, relationships among numbers, the relative magnitude of numbers, and skill in working with them. It is also an attitude that one can make sense of numbers. It includes the idea of "fluency" with numbers, that is, the ability to move easily and flexibly in the world of numbers. It also values *reasonableness* as an important component of doing mathematics.

We have observed that our students develop a powerful understanding of numbers that permits them to use numbers insightfully in many contexts. They enjoy partitioning numbers, exploring ways of representing numbers, considering relationships among numbers, and discussing number ideas.

Computational Strategies

Computation is one of the many components of number sense *and* strong number sense promotes learning to compute. Computation remains an important goal of mathematics programs. Yet as we emphasized sense-making and reasoning in our classrooms, we were concerned that computation be developed from the same perspective. We wanted children to develop understanding and think flexibly in this area, as well. Yet the question remained about how this might be accomplished, and we struggled to reconcile our traditional views of computation with new views.

Our backgrounds and narrow views of computation were part of the problem. In the past, computation often meant learning arbitrary rules for manipulating symbols. The work was *modeled by teachers*, rather than *processed by student*s. There was one acceptable way of finding an answer and classwork was driven by practice and accuracy. Computation tended to dominate the mathematics curriculum.

In the past, we viewed computation as distinct from the rest of the curriculum, requiring a different teaching approach. Now it is integrated into our total mathematics program. This change, however, was a gradual one.

Our students helped change our thinking, for *they* have a very different perspective. For them, computation is *not* memorizing and applying arbitrary rules. It is simply another aspect of problem solving to which one brings insight and number sense. It is more than skills—it is *doing mathematics*.

Some educators believe that computation is meaningful only if it has a real-world setting. However, we learned that a context isn't necessary. The students attack "naked computation" (i.e., 62 - 24) as a problem to solve. They invent a wide variety of procedures that draw upon their number sense.

To illustrate the number sense and computational strategies of children, several approaches to a problem are shown on the next two pages. Note the richness and diversity of their reasoning.

The children's work highlights that

- computation can be part of mathematics, rather than separate from it, and

- computation is part of children's emerging number sense and contributes to its development.

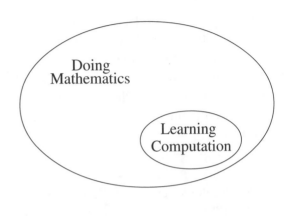

"Clearly, paper and pencil computation cannot continue to dominate the curriculum or there will be insufficient time for children to learn from each other, more important mathematics they need now and in the future."

NCTM 1989, 44

"How many second graders will be voting today?" was the question raised about the school's mock election one fall. There were two classrooms of 28 children in each one. The teacher said, "Can you figure the problem out on your own?"

Many strategies emerged. Since it was early in the year, some children modeled it with cubes. Then they started at 28 and counted 28 more (28, 29, 30, 31 . . .). There were also many mature strategies that showed good number sense.

The oral solutions included counting on by tens, front-end addition, using 25 as a nice number, and using the standard algorithm mentally.

There were several ways the children recorded their work, including "chunking" the numbers and the standard algorithm. Some children used such tools as base-ten blocks and the 100s chart.

Oral Methods

Well . . . I started with 28 and I counted by tens because it's easy for me to use tens. 28 and 10 more is 38 and 10 more is 48. Then, 8 more is 56.

2 and 2 is 4, so 20 and 20 is 40. 8 and 2 of the other 8 is 10. Then 50 and 6 more is 56.

8 and 8 is 16. I added the 1 with the 2 and 2, so it's 56.

I thought of it as money. 28¢ is a quarter and 3 pennies. Two quarters is 50¢. 6 pennies more is 56¢.

20 and 20 is 40. 8 and 8 is 16. 40 and 10 is 50 and 6 more is 56.

I took 2 from one of the 28s and put it with the other 28. That made 30. I still need to add 26. 30 and 26 is 56.

I started with 25 + 25 because I just know that. 25 and 25 is 50, 3 and 3 is 6. 50 and 6 is 56.

Written Methods

$$\begin{array}{r} 20 \\ +20 \\ \hline 40 \\ 16 \\ \hline 56 \end{array}$$

(8+8=16)

$$30+30=60$$
$$60-4=56$$

20 20 8 8

$$20+20=40$$
$$8+8=16$$
$$40+16=56$$

Learning Standard Algorithms

Many educators have concerns about the way standard algorithms have been taught in the past; some have questioned whether they should even be taught. Preoccupation with computation and traditional ways of teaching it have contributed to many children believing that mathematics is primarily memorizing rules for manipulating symbols. This is unfortunate and counterproductive, and we share the concerns that some raise about written computation.

Over the past three years, we have found that students do learn standard whole number computation, but in a very different way than in the past. We view the standard algorithms as *one* approach, not *the* approach. Perhaps this is a reason why this work is integrated into our curriculum without dominating or distorting it. A second reason may be that children *learn* written computation without our *teaching* it in the usual way.

We have found that the children often introduce standard algorithms along with their invented procedures. In discussions, they share their standard algorithm along with their other procedures. This may occur because of the familiarity with and understanding of numbers that children construct through emphasis on number sense and multiple computational strategies.

We enjoy watching standard algorithms unfold. Later in the year we attempt to have all second graders use them as well as their other approaches. This occurs without long explanations or extensive drill; it is a *product* of a problem-centered approach, rather than the *goal* of it. The algorithms are simply one more way to find an answer.

We also have observed and have data that children continue to use their own approaches and maintain their flexibility in computing after they have learned standard algorithms. We continue to emphasize that there is more than one option and encourage children to use the one that makes the most sense. As one student put it, they simply enjoy the "messing with numbers" that occurs as they use computational strategies.

It is widely accepted that written algorithms are important for children to learn. Since standard algorithms are so easily learned under a problem-centered approach, for several reasons it helps for children to have these skills as they move forward in school. We will revisit the learning of standard algorithms in the book's final section.

An Evolving Approach to Number Sense and Computational Strategies

We continually change as mathematics teachers the more we explore our new perspectives on teaching. This is particularly true with respect to our approach to traditional number concepts and computation. New approaches are implemented gradually; they do not happen quickly. It may help to understand the way our work has evolved over several years as you consider ways of changing your own teaching.

Stage 1: Initially, we had two mathematics programs—one that focused on mathematical reasoning and number sense and a second one that taught traditional skills. This latter work was done meaningfully, but tended to be independent of what was occurring within our problem-centered focus. (See diagram at right.)

There were at least two reasons for this. It was not clear initially how number concepts and computation developed under problem-centered approaches, and we wanted our students to understand place value, know basic facts, and compute with two-digit numbers. Society's high expectations in this area had shaped our beliefs about its importance.

Stage 2: As we gained experience with a problem-centered approach, we became aware that students were acquiring traditional content and skills through problems and seminars. Gradually, more number work was occurring in this context.

Yet we still felt that skills required additional attention and continued to set aside separate blocks of time for it. Nonetheless, we were starting to see a smoother fit. The dual program was becoming a unified one. (See diagram.)

Stage 3: Now, number sense and computational strategies are developed within the overall approach. (See diagram.) These ideas receive much attention throughout the year and we are continually learning new ways of helping children acquire them. When invented and traditional algorithms evolve throughout the year, we find that traditional algorithms are learned with far less teaching time and practice. Children also experience less stress.

We are pleased—our mathematics program is more cohesive and we teach important content in an ongoing manner that makes sense to children.

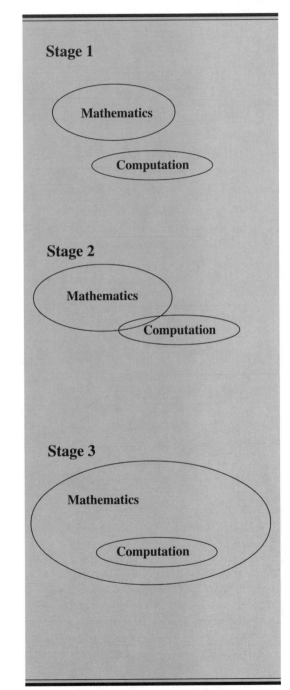

Summary of Approach to Developing Number Concepts and Computation

1. *Number and computation concepts are developed throughout the year.*

2. *Boundaries among operations, number concepts, and kinds of computation are removed.*

3. *Invented strategies emerge naturally and are emphasized throughout the year.*

4. *Standard algorithms are emphasized later in the year as another way to solve problems.*

Section 2

DEVELOPING NUMBER SENSE AND COMPUTATIONAL STRATEGIES

Chapter 5

A TEACHING PLAN

This section describes the way we organize and develop the curriculum for number sense and computational strategies. Our approach permits us to have a unified and consistent problem-centered curriculum. In particular, the instructional approach, which was presented in Section 1, remains the same. Key elements are summarized at left.

Before describing the way we organize and develop this work, it is important to first capture its components. There is an important agenda for numbers, operations, and computation in the primary grades that needs careful attention in mathematics programs. Key primary grade components are listed below.

Numbers
Meaning of numbers
Grouping and place value
Relationships among numbers
Relative magnitude of numbers
Intuitions and connections
Reading, writing, and comparing numbers
Ways of counting

Operations
Meaning of addition, subtraction, multiplication, and division
Recognizing situations appropriate to each operation
Solving problems

Computation
Using multiple strategies to compute
Knowing basic facts
Using invented strategies and standard algorithms

These topics are an integral part of what we mean by developing number sense and computational strategies. Children need to understand these ideas, make connections among the components, and develop proficiency with them.

The approach, which is described on the following pages, differs substantially from traditional practice. Typically, the content is organized into chapters, each topic is broken into small pieces, the pieces are arranged in hierarchical order and presented in a step-by-step fashion. Children's ideas, insights, and strategies receive minimal attention. Instruction is worksheet-driven with substantial time devoted to drill. While there may be attempts to develop meaning, the symbolic aspects dominate.

However, we have learned that instruction that focuses on mathematical thinking results in successful learning of concepts and skills by children of *all* abilities. The four major characteristics of our approach are described on the following pages.

Number computation and concepts are developed throughout the year.

Content is traditionally developed in chapters devoted to a single topic, such as "Facts to Ten," "Addition with Renaming," and "Exploring Multiplication." The chapter contains most of the work on the topic at that grade level. Further, each chapter is divided into "minichapters," that is, one or two lessons on each of several specific objectives with the expectation that each will be learned in one or two days. As a result there is a *very narrow* **window of opportunity** to learn.

Now our work on number and computation occurs throughout the year, receiving attention on many days in some form— as the focus of a lesson, as part of the daily warm-up, or as part of a discussion of a computational strategy.

This provides all children multiple opportunities throughout the year to develop understanding and mature strategies. Many children need this extended opportunity to assimilate content and ways of thinking. Multiple opportunities provide a *very wide* **window of opportunity** to learn.

Let's examine how children learn about subtraction. First, children encounter the operation in many settings with many types of problems. Some problems involve taking away, while others require children to find how many more, or compare two quantities. This is consistent with how they have encountered subtraction in out-of-school situations.

Children also use diverse strategies to find answers. For a problem involving 12 - 5, one child may use cubes. He counts out 12 cubes, takes away five of them, and then counts the seven remaining cubes.

O O O O O O O O̶ O̶ O̶ O̶ O̶
1 2 3 4 5 6 7 8 9 10 11 12

Another child mentally counts back from 12 to 7 (*"12 . . . 11, 10, 9, 8, 7"*) holding up a finger each time the next number is said until she has five fingers showing.

A third child reasons, *"12 take away 2 is 10, take away 3 more to get 7."* A fourth child's strategy uses addition and doubles: *"6 and 6 is 12, so 7 and 5 is 12."*

These approaches emerged during one discussion and reveal the different ways the children are thinking, as well as their levels of mathematical maturity. Our teachers have learned that it likely will take several weeks and many experiences before some children shift to more mature strategies. We have learned that shifts in the way children think occur gradually.

> *"We argue that disadvantaged children, like all children, can begin their educational life by engaging in active thinking and problem solving. We argue further that when thinking-oriented instruction is carefully organized for this purpose, children can acquire the traditional basic skills in the process of reasoning and solving problems. As a result, they can acquire not only the fundamentals of a discipline but also the ability to apply those fundamentals, and—critically—a belief in their own capacities as learners and thinkers."*
>
> Resnick et al. 1991, 28

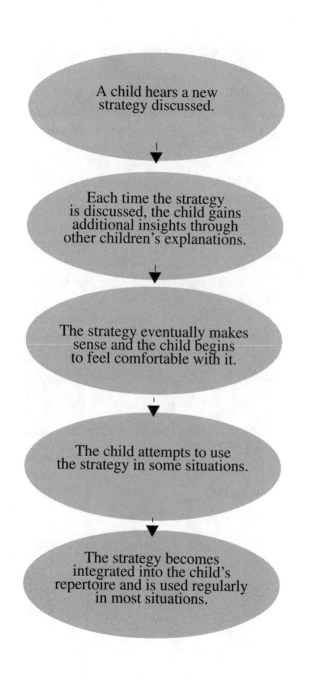

A child hears a new strategy discussed.

Each time the strategy is discussed, the child gains additional insights through other children's explanations.

The strategy eventually makes sense and the child begins to feel comfortable with it.

The child attempts to use the strategy in some situations.

The strategy becomes integrated into the child's repertoire and is used regularly in most situations.

The flow chart at left suggests a path for learning strategies. This approach reinforces earlier discussions about allowing children to make sense of ideas in their own way and on their own schedule.

Traditional approaches appear *efficient;* however, we have learned that developing content and strategies throughout the year is far more *effective.* Not only does it result in greater learning, it is also more efficient because less time is needed for reteaching.

This approach places new responsibilities on teachers. We need to (1) be aware of major ideas at a grade level, (2) use tasks that involve these ideas, and (3) create opportunities for discussing them. This may seem complex, but it is not difficult as one gains experience and confidence.

Boundaries among operations, number concepts, and kinds of computation are removed.

This characteristic follows naturally from the previous one. The organization of traditional programs places boundaries around the content. Two-digit numbers are developed before three-digit numbers; addition is presented before subtraction; written computation with no renaming occurs before computation with naming;

and written computation precedes oral computation. Our experience has led us to remove the following boundaries:

Boundaries among operations. Problems involving the four operations occur regularly. On many days, students encounter more than one operation as well as multistep problems involving two operations.

Children interpret these problems in terms of the action implied or their prior experience with similar situations. To solve the problems, they make use of their counting knowledge.

Boundaries among number concepts. We no longer focus on numbers to 20 until November in Grade 1 and two-digit numbers until January in Grade 2. One-, two-, and three-digit numbers occur throughout the year as they arise in problems and tasks. We take advantage of each opportunity to focus on numeration concepts and skills. Thus, much place value work occurs in seminar discussions.

Fraction ideas are treated similarly. They arise frequently in various contexts; these situations then are used to develop fraction concepts. Consequently, fractions are discussed several times during the year and the discussions are supplemented with tasks that provide further experience.

Boundaries among kinds of computation. Our children regularly (a) compute with basic facts and multi-digit numbers, (b) do both mental and written computation, and (c) compute without consideration of whether or not the computation involves renaming. They may use all kinds or aspects of computation in a single lesson.

This approach is very different than the one we had been accustomed to. By removing boundaries we allow for integrating these ideas in our curriculum. The result is improved and connected learning for *all* children.

When boundaries are removed, children develop a feeling of power and a sense of the generality of strategies. In particular, they apply "basic fact" strategies to larger numbers. Some strategies are better learned with larger numbers. For example, it may be easier to see the value of counting on for $48 + 2$ than for $8 + 2$. For $8 + 2$, some children find it just as easy to *count all* as to *count on*.

Invented strategies emerge naturally and are emphasized throughout the year.

In Grade 1, invented strategies become commonplace about December, when children's problems and tasks more frequently involve larger numbers. In Grade 2, they begin early in the year. At both levels, these strategies, which evolve from children's work with numbers, are regularly emphasized. See the example at right.

Invented procedures are closely linked to children's number sense and mathematical reasoning. The methods involve breaking numbers apart in ways that demonstrate understanding and also fit the computational situation.

Not only are children's methods a part of their number sense, they also are a major means by which children *expand* their number sense. As first and second grade children regularly group and partition numbers, we notice that they become more flexible in their thinking. For many children, this work is a form of mathematical "play." As one child stated, "I enjoy messing with numbers."

Many of children's invented procedures involve place value ideas that underlie standard written algorithms. Often, the only difference is the sequence of the steps and the way the work is recorded. Children's experiences with invented procedures become the foundation for learning and understanding standard algorithms.

A Child's Invented Strategy

A problem that a child had created involved finding 3 seventeens. One child thought,

"20 and 20 and 20 is 60. That is too large because I used 20 instead of 17. So, I need to subtract 3 three times. The answer is 51."

The other children were excited and soon they were creating other examples to which they could apply this strategy.

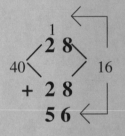

A Child's Standard Algorithm

Diana thought as follows for 28 + 28:

$$1$$
$$28$$
$$40 \diagdown \diagup 16$$
$$+\ 28$$
$$56$$

*"I added 8 and 8, but I can't write 16 below the line because the answer [i.e., 416] wouldn't make sense. So, I wrote the **6** and put the **10** with the 20s. Then I added 1, 2, and 2 which gave me 50 and wrote the 5 next to the 6."*

Standard algorithms are emphasized later in the year as another way to solve problems.

Although standard algorithms are not typically part of the Grade 1 curriculum, nonetheless we see some children begin to use them by the last quarter of the year. This is an outgrowth of their work with invented strategies.

Early in Grade 2, standard algorithms are often introduced by children during our seminars. As with all children's approaches, we discuss standard algorithms as one of many strategies. We may ask other children whether it makes sense or why it works. When children record their work symbolically, their methods are often similar to the standard algorithm (see the example at left).

Later in the year, we give more attention to standard algorithms and help children use them insightfully. Their work throughout the year causes them to have a strong understanding of place value and algorithms. As a result they learn these algorithms without stress or extensive drill. Even after most children learn the algorithms, we continue to emphasize many approaches and we are pleased that children continue to use their own methods.

Summary

We have described where our commitment to sense-making has led with respect to teaching arithmetic. The way we teach now is very different from the way we taught a few years ago. Throughout, we have learned from observing our students. As their learning changed, so did our teaching, and as our teaching continues to change, so does their learning.

A major advantage of our approach is that it links teaching for understanding and teaching for skills within a single framework. Thinking of arithmetic as developing number sense and computational strategies has helped us approach arithmetic as part of mathematics. No longer is it necessary to have two curricula or ignore one aspect of mathematics to focus on the other. Yet we know that we must work at developing fluency and proficiency. It doesn't just happen.

How Many Days in Two Years?

$$365 + 365$$

$$300 + 300 = 600$$

$$600 + 60 = 660$$

$$660 + 30 = 690$$

$$690 + 10 = 700$$

$$700 + 20 = 720$$

$$720 + 5 + 5 = 730$$

So, $365 + 365 = 730$

Chapter 6

CHILDREN'S COMPUTATIONAL STRATEGIES

We continually have been impressed by the problem solving and computational strategies that children create. Both types of strategies emerge naturally from their encounters with mathematics in various contexts and the number sense they have developed. Their strategies are not the result of direct instruction.

In this section we will highlight and briefly discuss some of the most common computational strategies that children invent for working with larger numbers. Their strategies are clearly problem solving tools; that is, they help children find solutions to problems. Many examples of their approaches have been displayed throughout the book. Pages 52 and 53, for example, present several examples of children's strategies and the diverse ways they think.

Some sources refer to children's computational strategies as "mental computation." We prefer the term "invented strategies" as we believe it communicates more clearly the nature of their work, while avoiding limitations and ambiguities of the other term.

Strategies often emerge as children explain their thinking during seminars. When a child shares a strategy, all children have the opportunity to learn about it. As it is discussed, children learn how it works and have the chance to try it for themselves.

We have also learned to have children record their thinking using words and/or number sentences. The written record highlights the mathematical ideas, helps them clarify their thinking, and promotes retention. "Chunking" notation, shown on the next page, is a clear and manageable way of showing one's thinking. This notation is popular among both first and second graders.

Several types of strategies are described and illustrated on the following pages. This presentation attempts to acquaint readers with the main strategies that children use and the underlying mathematical ideas involved. This knowledge can help each of us as we work with children.

The richness and diversity of children's thinking is inherent in the examples. Notice the strong number sense, understanding of fundamental concepts and relationships, and the mature counting strategies displayed. Additionally, the Notes for Teachers section provides ideas for linking the strategies to important concepts and skills.

Partitioning numbers by tens and ones is one of the most common strategies. The diagram below illustrates the partitioning of 39 and 16.

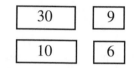

30	9
10	6

The oral names for two-digit numbers may encourage this strategy as, for example, "thirty-six" suggests two parts, a "thirty" part and a "six" part. This may explain why young children can use it prior to any tens and ones instruction.

Children use the following steps:

1. Partition both numbers

2. Add the tens (often done first) and add the ones

3. Add the two partial sums

Oral Example

39 + 16

*Well, first I added the 30 and the
10. Then, I added the 9 and the 6.
9 and 6 is . . . 15. Then, I added the
10 from the 15 to 40 and added 5 more.*

Recorded Examples

39 + 16

Approach 1

$$30 + 10 = 40$$
$$9 + 6 = 15$$
$$40 + 10 = 50$$
$$50 + 2 = 52$$

Approach 2

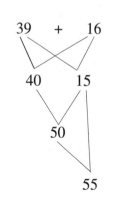

Use the children's discussion as an opportunity to conduct minilessons about

• Tens and ones
• Adding tens

Have a child use base-ten blocks to justify the thinking and explain it to others.

See if any children use the following variation for subtraction. For 43 - 24, a child might think "43 - 23" and subtract 40 - 20 and 3 - 3. Then the child subtracts the extra 1.

Some children extend this strategy to 3 or more addends. For 24 + 24 + 24 you might hear: "3 twenties make 60. 4 and 4 and 4 is 12. 60 and 12 is 72."

Counting On/Back from a Number

When using the "counting on" or "counting back" strategy, one number is the starting point. Partitions of the second number are added to it. Counting on is also used in subtraction situations where one counts from the part to the whole. The difference is the answer. Counting back can also be used for subtracting. In this case, one counts back starting with the whole.

There are several ways in which students work with one of the numbers. They often partition it so they can count by tens or fives (see below).

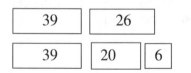

The "Counting On/Back" strategy is implemented in a variety of ways. These methods require strong number sense and flexibility in adapting the approach to the numbers involved.

Oral Examples _____

39 + 26

I counted on from 39 by tens in my head. I went 39 . . . 49 . . . 59. Then I added 6 more. 59 and 6 is 65.

69 + 14

I took 1 from the 14 and added it to 69. Next, I added 10 to get 80. Then I added 80 and 3.

83 - 18

83 minus 3 is 80. Take away 10 more . . . that's 70. I still have to subtract 5 . . . so, 65.

Recorded Examples _____

25 + 15

25, 30, 35, 40. I counted by five.

$2.00 - $1.35

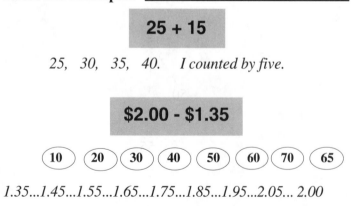

1.35...1.45...1.55...1.65...1.75...1.85...1.95...2.05... 2.00

Counting on and back from a number is promoted by familiarity with the hundreds chart. (See pages 96–99 or ways of working with the chart.)

This strategy provides the opportunity to introduce, further develop, and reinforce skill with counting by fives and tens in a purposeful context.

Notice that the student wrote 10, 20, 30 . . . above each sum. This allowed her to keep track of how much she had counted on.

Using "Nice Numbers"

"Nice numbers" refers to numbers that are easy for children to work with. For example, it is much easier to add 30 to 65 than it is to add 28 to 65.

Nice numbers are often multiples of 10 or numbers like 25 which are easy to work with because of their connection to money. Familiar doubles are often considered nice numbers; it is easier to add 25 and 25, for example, than it is to add 27 and 27.

The strategy makes use of partitioning in a somewhat different way, as illustrated below for 67 + 28. When replacing 28 with 30, the child is aware that 30 is made up of the parts 28 and 2.

67	28
67	30

Oral Examples _____

I know that 25 and 25 is 50. I still need to add 4 more. 50 plus 4 is 54.

67 + 28

It's easier to add 30. 67 plus 30 is 97. But 97 is 2 too large, since I only needed to add 28. So I must take 2 from 97 to get 95.

70 - 19

70 minus 20 is 50. Since I subtracted 20 instead of 19 . . . I had to add one back. So it's 51.

Recorded Examples _____

$$\$1.35 + \underline{\quad} = \$2.00$$

$$\$1.30 + .70 = \$2.00$$

$$\$1.35 + .65 = \$2.00$$

Once this strategy is introduced, the other children often become excited and try to create other problems that can be solved by this strategy.

"Nice numbers" are often used in problems involving equal addends or multiplication, as described on pages 71 and 72.

This student felt it was easy to begin by using $1.30 instead of $1.35. She then realized that if the starting number was $1.35, then 70¢ would be 5¢ too large and changed it to 65¢.

Translating to a New Problem

A less common, but powerful, strategy used by some children is to replace the given numbers with ones that are more manageable.

In the first example shown at the right, the student changed 25 + 15 into 20 + 20 and added using the new numbers. The approach involves the idea of "compensation." That is, when one addend is decreased by 5, increasing the other addend by 5 compensates for this.

This translation strategy is related to the nice number strategy. The goal of creating a new, easier example is to use numbers that are "nice" to work with.

The strategy clearly involves many components of number sense, such as a strong understanding of number relationships and multiple ways of partitioning numbers.

Oral Examples

25 + 15

I took the 5 off the 25 and I put it on the 15 and I know they both were 20. 20 plus 20 equals 40.

49 + 51

It's 100. I just changed it to 50 + 50.

59 + 28 + 17

Student: What's 90 + 14?

Teacher: What's 90 + 10?

Student: Oh, that's 100, so it's 104.

Teacher: How did you do that?

Student: First, I changed it to 60 + 27 + 17.
Then I changed it to 60 + 30 + 14.
I knew that 60 and 30 was 90,
so I just had to add 14 more.

Recorded Examples

25 + 15

25 - 5 = 20
15 + 5 = 20
20 + 20 = 40

The use of this strategy can often be seen in work with basic facts. When faced with 7 + 9, some children use 8 + 8 instead; other children might change it to 10 + 6. Thus, fact work sets the stage for the use of the strategies with larger numbers.

Translation often occurs in situations where it is natural to use doubles or multiples of ten.

The "number of the day" routine promotes the use of compensation as children build on the responses of others. One child, for example, might suggest 100 - 75 as a name for 25. This becomes the basis for later suggestions like 200 - 175 and 300 - 275. To another student it might suggest 99 - 74.

Children's strategies for two-digit numbers are the building blocks for adding and subtracting larger numbers. They also are the foundation for solving problems involving equal parts—that is, multiplication and division problems.

Children view multiplication problems in terms of repeated addition and list the addends as shown at the right. These problems are often student-initiated. They enjoy creating and solving these everyday problems. They may find

- the number of hours in a week,

- the number of six-packs 8 children bring to school for a can drive,

- the amount of money collected for a field trip if each child brings 25¢,

A common approach is to "chunk" the addends to make "nice" or manageable numbers as shown at right.

There are 9 classrooms in the building. One is empty. In each room there are 7 windows. How many windows in all?

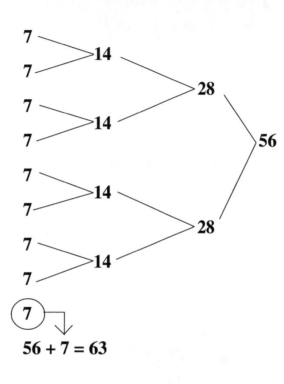

56 + 7 = 63

Note: Successive doubling was used. Then the "extra" 7 was added to 56.

How many hours are there in a week?

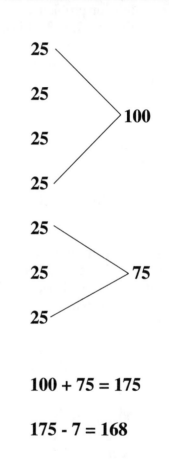

100 + 75 = 175

175 - 7 = 168

Note: 25 was used instead of 24, because it was a nice number. After grouping 25s to get 175, the child then subtracted the 7 extra ones.

Children's use of equal addends is also the basis for solving division problems. Thus, sharing 60 pennies among 3 children involves finding a number that fits the 3 equal partitions of 60, as illustrated by the diagram below.

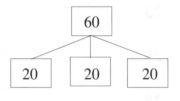

In the first problem at right, children recognized that three 50s is 150. Then they split each 50 into two equal parts of 25. This gave them 6 parts in all.

The second problem involves two people sharing 250 marbles. Note the two steps used to solve it.

For sharing $5.00 among 4 people, a similar method is used. Many children see a connection between dividing a number into 4 equal parts and the idea of 1/4 of a number.

We had 150 cookies and we had 6 friends over. They all took some cookies until they each got the same amount. How many did they each get?

"They each get 25 because 150 ÷ 3 = 50 and 50 ÷ 2 = 25.

So do that with each 50 and we each get 25."

Two children decided to share 250 marbles between them. How many did each one get?

"We know that 100 + 100 = 200. There are 50 left. So we tried 25. 25 and 25 is 50. Each one got 125 marbles."

Four children found a 5-dollar bill. They decided to share it equally. How much money did they each get?

"We gave everyone $1.00. Then we tried 50¢ more. That was too much. So, we tried 25¢ and that worked. Each one got 1 dollar and 1 quarter ($1.25)."

We have included the fraction work on these pages to show where children's understanding of numbers can lead. Primary teachers often include exploratory experiences with fraction concepts using materials such as pattern blocks and circles cut in halves, fourths, and eighths.

One activity is creating designs and finding the amount they represent. Children naturally want to record their work and thus write number sentences that use fractions. This lets them show "how smart they are." However, they are not formally *computing*; rather, they are combining fraction parts using the picture as the basis. They also use their ability to count by various fractions (1/8, 2/8, 3/8 . . .), as well as their knowledge of fraction relationships. They do make use of strategies they have learned, including "chunking" and representing a quantity in more than one way.

The examples on this page came from a pattern-block task. In both examples, the children found the amount represented by their design when the hexagon is the whole (1 unit).

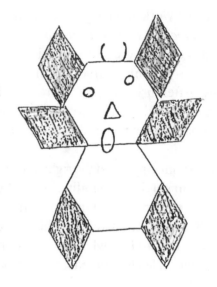

$$\frac{18}{6} = 3$$

$$3 + 4 = 7$$

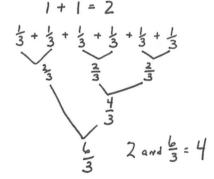

The student work at the right was motivated by *Ed Emberley's Picture Pie,* a book that illustrates designs created from circles that have been cut into halves, fourths, and eighths. After discussing his work, the children then made designs. Most of them want to write number sentences that use fractions.

The classroom vignette at the right illustrates the problem solving capabilities of children who have a deep understanding of fraction concepts and fraction relationships. Note that it was the student who chose to pursue this problem. He also solved it without adult intervention.

My students were working on the problem of sharing 28 cupcakes evenly. I noticed Truman was trying to share using 16 people, but was struggling. I commented, "I don't think it's going to work."

I thought he would try another number, but he kept working. I finally heard him say, "I've got it!" I walked to his desk doubting that he was successful. But he had done it!

His thinking was, *"Well, I gave 16 people 1 cupcake and I subtracted 28 - 16 = 12. Sooooo . . . , I cut 8 cupcakes in half, and gave 16 people 1/2 cupcake. That made 4 cupcakes left, soooo . . . , I cut the last 4 cupcakes into 4 equal pieces and gave 16 people 1/4 of a cupcake and had none left over."*

I asked how much each person got. *"Well, each will get 1 whole, 1/2, and 1/4. Now, if you draw a circle and draw lines through it you will see that 2/4 = 1/2, and if you add 2/4 to 1/4 you'll get 3/4, soooo.... each person will get 1 and 3/4 cupcakes, and IT'S EVEN!"* He was so proud!!

Marla Wehrle
McKinstry Elementary School

$$\frac{1}{8} + \frac{1}{8} + \frac{1}{8} + \frac{1}{8} = \frac{4}{8}$$

$$\frac{4}{8} = \frac{1}{2}$$

$$\frac{1}{8} + \frac{1}{8} + \frac{1}{8} + \frac{1}{8} + \frac{1}{8} + \frac{1}{4} = \frac{7}{8}$$

$$\frac{5}{8} + \frac{1}{4} = \frac{7}{8}$$

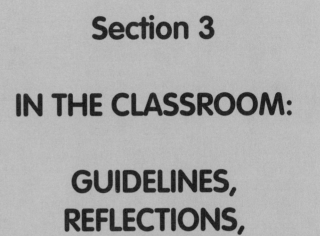

Section 3

IN THE CLASSROOM:

GUIDELINES, REFLECTIONS, IDEAS

Introduction to Section 3

This section presents guidelines, reflections, and ideas for implementing the approach to number sense and computational strategies that was presented in Section 2. It contains specific teaching ideas as well as insights based on our experiences that might help other teachers. There are four parts:

- launching a new year,

- dealing with basic facts,

- using tools: hundreds charts and base-ten blocks, and

- developing standard algorithms.

Launching a New Year

It doesn't matter how long we've been teaching this way—whether it's the first year or the tenth year. Each fall we face the same challenges of getting started with a new group of students. What we remember most clearly is what last year's students could do in May; what we don't remember as clearly is what we did to bring them to that point. As one teacher reflected:

When school begins in August, I'm always a little nervous. I wonder what skills my new students will bring with them. I find it difficult to remember what beginning second grade students can do. I remember vividly the mature strategies which students had developed by the end of the year.

The students understood and felt comfortable with numbers, developed number relationships, and learned strategies for computing. In other words, they had number sense and computational strategies.

As I contemplate this approaching school year, three important goals for me are assessing what they know, carefully planning initial work, and establishing a community of learners.

Sue Weinberg
Dike Elementary School

There are so many things we need to consider beyond the mathematics at this time. We must accept that these students *will* be different from last year's students. While they will likely arrive at the same endpoint, we know the paths they travel will be different. It is clear to us that what we do in the early days sets the stage for the whole year. These ideas are captured in the following reflection:

As I teach mathematics, one of my important roles is to establish an atmosphere of acceptance to all contributions. Every idea, question, and strategy must be respected by all members of our community, for I know how important it is to create an environment in which students feel safe sharing their ideas. I also must remember that all children will learn in their own time and in their own ways. All of this reminds me of the importance of being patient, perseverant, and persistent.

Christina Hartman,
Cedar Heights Elementary School

At the beginning of the year, then, both mathematics and how children encounter mathematics must be considered. It is in this context that children's number sense and computational strategies emerge.

Note: Section 1, Chapter 3, discusses several important aspects of a problem-centered approach and the work of teachers, including questions about how to get started.

Launching Mathematics as Part of Exploring a New Environment

A new grade level . . . a new classroom . . . a new teacher . . . some new classmates . . . a new desk . . . new expectations . . . new routines . . . new school supplies . . . a new schedule . . .

There's a lot going on the first few days. Teachers know they need to help children feel comfortable in their new world and plan appropriate activities. This involves getting to know one another, getting to know the classroom, and starting to build a learning environment.

We have learned that many tasks address important mathematics as well as our broader goals. These tasks can help us learn about our students' mathematical backgrounds.

Collecting and organizing data about individuals leads to building information about the community of children who will be learning and working together for the school year. Both first and second grade teachers have found that an early focus on data has been highly beneficial. In particular, it is an excellent way of assessing children's knowledge of numbers and their ability to solve problems.

Data collection and graphing is discussed in the first box on the next page. This is followed by two additional experiences that also fit the purposes of these.

"Establishing a community of learners—that is, developing a group climate that supports thinking and sharing thinking, values the ideas of others, and encourages risk taking and learning from others—is the primary agenda each fall. We know that establishing our mathematical community will take time—sometimes a few weeks and sometimes two or three months; we also know that it will occur.

We work hard at building this community and each fall we have to remind ourselves of the complexity of this task. Each of us has had classes that moved fairly quickly in becoming a mathematical community and each of us of has had classes that had much greater difficulty and took more time."

From the discussion on page 39 dealing with establishing a mathematical community.

Learning About Us

How many children have birthdays in March? four letters in their first names? brothers and sisters? pets? These questions can launch data collection activities resulting in graphs about birthdays, about numbers of letters in first names, about number of brothers and sisters, about numbers of pets.

These graphs provide a class "picture" or profile and lead naturally to solving problems—*about, most, least, the same as, how many more or less, and so on.* Children have begun the process of solving problems and sharing their thinking.

In some first grade classrooms, children work in pairs to select a question for which to collect information. Each pair then decides how to display their results. Presentations of children's work leads to discussions about ways of representing data. The approach helps children learn that data is more than numbers or graphs—it can tell a story about the children.

Extensions can involve finding the number of eyes and fingers in a class, leading to counting by 2s, 5s, and 10s.

Comparing Classes

It is a natural extension to look at the number of boys and girls in their classroom. One class found the following:

12 boys
10 girls
22 in all

A discussion led to how this might compare to the class next door. Two children collected the data and reported:

9 boys
15 girls
24 in all

Many questions arose. Which room had the most girls? the most boys? How many more girls are there in one room than the other room?

One child said, "I think there are 25 girls in all." Then all children became involved in checking her solution.

Again, collecting data has led to problem solving and mathematical reasoning in an everyday context. Children are working together and sharing their thinking—a mathematical community is slowly growing.

Forming Groups

"Boys and girls, there are 23 of us. Sometimes we will work with a partner. How many groups of children will there be?"

Children can act this out, and then make drawings or use objects to find the solution. The discussion includes dealing with the "extra person."

Children can then explore the related problems of working in groups of three or four. They can work with a partner to solve the new problem.

Exploring Manipulatives

Getting acquainted with the classroom can include *getting acquainted* with the tools for learning mathematics.

Each day, time can be spent in small groups exploring a different manipulative. The children are free to use the materials to build, sort, or make designs. We have found that this initial experience helps children use manipulatives appropriately when solving problems.

Calendar Math Activities

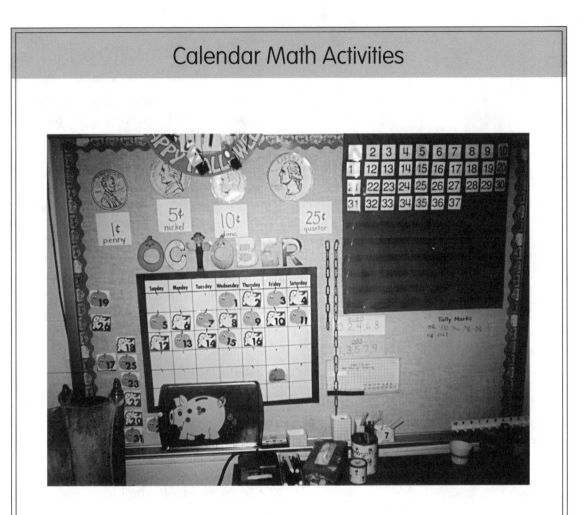

The morning routine involves a great deal of mathematics. Children identify the day of the month, the number of days in school, the amount of money for the day in school, and a variety of other ideas. As the photo shows, the hundreds chart is being constructed one day at a time, tally marks are emphasized, and odd and even numbers are highlighted.

Launching Daily Routines

We have been greatly impressed with the power of daily routines for helping children develop number concepts, relationships, computational strategies, and other skills. When used thoughtfully, they provide the opportunity for rich mathematical discussions. Through routines, children have sustained contact with ideas. They also anticipate the work and mentally prepare for it. The work is like an ongoing conversation occurring over many days. These routines can be established early and built on throughout the year.

Routines enable teachers

- to provide ongoing maintenance;

- to develop topics, such as time and money, throughout the year;

- to pose everyday problems; and

- to help children extend their thinking about numbers.

"Calendar math," for example, can be a valuable routine, and include work with counting, money, patterns, number sequence, odd and even numbers, multiples of a number, and problem solving. (Page 28 provides further discussion of this work.) The photograph on the previous page shows one approach to it.

Several teachers effectively use the "number of the day" routine. Children suggest a multitude of ways of expressing that number. Often the number of days the children have been in school is used, that is, on the 12th day of school the number is 12.

Over time, children show great growth with this task and make use of patterns in their expressions. For example, one child might suggest 30 - 18 for 12 after hearing another contribute 20 - 8. Their ideas show good number sense and use many computational strategies. The complexity of their ideas also builds; new ideas emerge, such as multiplication and division. The two panels on the following page relate to this work.

Teachers also encourage children to use mathematical language to describe relationships among numbers. For example, 24 is

a lot *bigger than* 5,
4 *more than* 20,
1 *less than* 25,
the *double* of 12,
about half of 50,
between 20 and 25,
almost halfway from 20 to 30,
an *even* number.

Number of the Day

50

$10 + 10 + 10 + 10 + 10$

$20 + 20 + 10$

$25 + 25$

$1/2 \text{ of } 100$

$49 + 1$

$5 + 5 + 5 + \ldots + 5 + 5 + 5$

$100 - 50$

$48 + 2$

$45 + 5$

25×2

$60 - 10$

$15 + 15 + 15 + 5$

5×10

$42 + 8$

$35 + 15$

$20 + 10 + 10 + 10$

$55 - 5$

$57 - 7$

Number of the Week

Some teachers use a "number of the week" rather than a "number of the day." One teacher explained her reasons for a number of the week as follows:

"Using the same number for an entire week allows less mature students to think about the number, listen to other students, have more time to prepare a response, and participate when they are ready.

"When I used a new number each day, these students did not have the time they needed to reflect on the number in order to contribute. Consequently, they usually lost interest in the task."

Marla Wehrle,
McKinstry Elementary School,
Waterloo

She begins by posting a number on chart paper. Students write down ideas for that number on slips of paper that they place in a small basket. A few slips are drawn each day to be discussed, validated, and written on the chart. New slips are added each day.

Launching a "Big Mathematical Idea"

Much of the content of elementary school mathematics can be organized around a few "big ideas." These key ideas serve as unifying themes for many topics and skills.

One such idea is that a number (or "whole") can be expressed in terms of its parts in many ways. Resnick describes this idea as "additive composition" (see left column). This is illustrated below.

whole			
part		part	
part	part	part	part
part		part	part

Additive composition underlies both addition and subtraction, as well as highlights their relationship. Adding involves finding the whole when the parts are known, whereas subtraction involves finding one part when the whole and the other part are known. All four operations can be described in terms of parts (or equal parts) and wholes.

Facility in partitioning numbers helps children develop their number sense. They become more aware of relationships among numbers and begin to use various ways of thinking both *with* and *about* numbers. This work also contributes to the development of patterns and computational strategies, and ultimately supports the learning of skills.

It is important to launch this idea early in the year so that children become familiar with it and build on it. There are numerous activities that contribute to part-part-whole thinking for both first and second grade children. First grade teachers have been particularly impressed with the value of emphasizing partitioning in developing more mature ways of thinking.

The next five examples present tasks that involve partitioning. We have found these to be highly productive ones that work well at the beginning of the year. The "tens frame" activity, in particular, has helped children shift from counting individual objects to being able to quickly recognize partitions of ten and other numbers. It also launches a focus on computational strategies for basic facts.

Exploring Partitions of Numbers

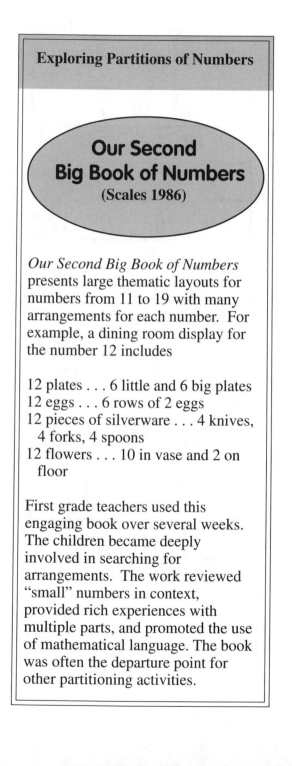

Our Second Big Book of Numbers
(Scales 1986)

Our Second Big Book of Numbers presents large thematic layouts for numbers from 11 to 19 with many arrangements for each number. For example, a dining room display for the number 12 includes

12 plates . . . 6 little and 6 big plates
12 eggs . . . 6 rows of 2 eggs
12 pieces of silverware . . . 4 knives, 4 forks, 4 spoons
12 flowers . . . 10 in vase and 2 on floor

First grade teachers used this engaging book over several weeks. The children became deeply involved in searching for arrangements. The work reviewed "small" numbers in context, provided rich experiences with multiple parts, and promoted the use of mathematical language. The book was often the departure point for other partitioning activities.

12 Ways to Get 11

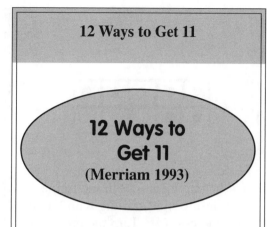

12 Ways to Get 11
(Merriam 1993)

12 Ways to Get 11 provides another opportunity to children to explore the myriad ways of partitioning numbers. Each of the 12 thematic layouts shows a way of making 11.

Examples include "Three sets of triplets in baby carriages and a pair of twins in the stroller," and in a mailbox, "seven letters, two packages, a mail-order catalog, and a picture postcard."

A natural follow up is to have the children create their own version of a way to make 11 or some other number using a familiar context, such as the school playground or classroom.

Some teachers have each child contribute a page to a class book entitled, *20 Ways to Get 12*.

A Pattern Block Activity

In this activity children make a pattern block design using a specified number of blocks. A first experience might involving making a design with 6 blocks. The children then indicate how many of each kind of block was used.

The above design uses 1 hexagon, 2 parallelograms, and 3 triangles. Another design might use 2 hexagons, 2 trapezoids, and 2 triangles. The results can be recorded by the teacher so that children see the many ways of representing 6. A natural extension, often suggested by the children, is to write number sentences for each pattern.

Such experiences help children learn multiple partitions of numbers, rather then viewing them as collections of ones.

The Tens Frame

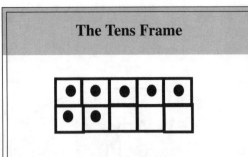

Place counters on a grid on the overhead projector. Fill the frame from left to right starting with the top row and cover it. Turn the projector on and remove the cover for two brief viewings (2–3 seconds each). Ask, "How many counters are there?" Remove the cover to let the children check their responses.

Have them describe their thinking. For 7 counters, one child thought, "7 . . . because there are 2 more than 5." Another child noted, "7 . . . because it's 3 less than 10."

Children learn to recognize 7 and 3, as well as other pairs, as partitions of 10 without counting. The activity also promotes using 5 and 10 as benchmarks. This is particularly the case when the number of counters is between 10 and 20, and 2 tens frames are used.

The "tens frame" activity, found in many resources, is most effective when used as a daily routine.

Find the Part

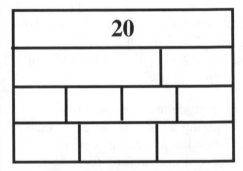

Second grade teachers have used this task early in the year. Various partitions of 20 are shown above. One or more parts are given and children must find the missing part. More complex examples evolve over the course of the year.

Once children are familiar with the task, the chart can show just the size of the parts. The children must use the relative size of the boxes to determine possible solutions.

Solving and discussing solutions to problems is the heart of our work—and the process needs to begin on day one. At the beginning of Grade 1, problems arise from data collection activities or everyday classroom settings. Other sources include teacher-posed problems and children's books.

Rooster's Off to See the World and *Miss Spider's Tea Party* are examples of counting books that lead to problem solving at this time. A page in the latter book was a springboard for a problem about the number of teacups needed if 3 spiders were having tea and there was a cup for every "hand."

The three examples on the following pages were used early in second grade. The first problem arises from a discussion of school supplies. The second problem, Kelsey's Problem, was posed on the eleventh day. It is important to get children involved in creating problems—and the sooner the better. These types of problems usually take about 10 minutes to solve and discuss. The discussion needs to highlight both the mathematics and the children's strategies.

The third problem is an example of an extended problem which is based on the book *10 Black Dots*. Children need to solve all kinds of problems—little problems, medium-sized problems, and big problems. We have learned that children enjoy challenging problems early in the year that may last more than one day.

After reading the book, the children decided to create their own *10 Black Dots* books. Children illustrate the books using 1 dot for page 1, 2 dots for page 2, etc. The teacher posed the problem of how many dots each child would need. This meant they needed to find the sum of the numbers from 1 through 10 (see page 85).

The second part of the problem involves finding how many dots the teacher must buy for the whole class, in this case 20 students (see page 86). Both parts illustrate children's wide variety of strategies as well as their number sense and resourcefulness. The seminars presented opportunities for teachers to highlight various ways of counting, patterns, and place value.

Note: Section 1, Chapter 3, contains an extended discussion on using problems and sources of problems. See pages 27 to 39.

School Supplies

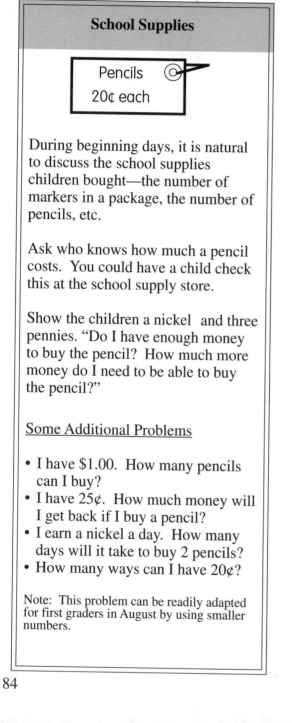

Pencils
20¢ each

During beginning days, it is natural to discuss the school supplies children bought—the number of markers in a package, the number of pencils, etc.

Ask who knows how much a pencil costs. You could have a child check this at the school supply store.

Show the children a nickel and three pennies. "Do I have enough money to buy the pencil? How much more money do I need to be able to buy the pencil?"

Some Additional Problems

- I have $1.00. How many pencils can I buy?
- I have 25¢. How much money will I get back if I buy a pencil?
- I earn a nickel a day. How many days will it take to buy 2 pencils?
- How many ways can I have 20¢?

Note: This problem can be readily adapted for first graders in August by using smaller numbers.

Kelsey's Problem

"I have 11¢. Tootsie Rolls cost 2¢ each. How many Tootsie Rolls can I buy? How much money will I have left over?"

Kelsey read her problem to her classmates, who were seated on the floor. Each child worked with a partner for 2 minutes. Before sharing solutions, the children were reminded that their classmates were going to be their teachers and that they needed to listen carefully.

Phil and Carl, who presented first, thought about 2 nickels and a penny. They knew that they could get 2 candies with each nickel and have a penny left over each time (see below). Then they explained they took the two extra pennies and bought another candy. And there would still be 1¢ left over. The teacher summarized their approach to help the children reflect on it.

The next pair of children counted by 2s, holding up 1 finger each time.

The third group also counted by twos, showing two fingers each time, explaining that each pair meant 1 Tootsie Roll.

The teacher then asked what number sentence might be written. Maria wrote:

11 - 10 = 1

After the class discussed what each of the numbers meant in terms of the problem, the teacher asked for other number sentences. Billy suggested they could take 2 away from 11 each time, and Rachel talked about adding 2 each time. She wrote:

2 + 2 + 2 + 2 + 2 = 10

To conclude the discussion, the teacher asked how many twos are in 10. The children realized that *5 twos* is 10, and a delightful mathematical exploration came to a close.

Note: On day 19, the problem was: *I have 19¢ and I want to buy some cotton candy. It costs $1.00. How much more money do I need?* The problems were becoming more complex.

Approach 1

Kitty Cat counters were used to represent the problem. Then the objects were counted to get 55 dots in all.

Approach 2

Dots were drawn to represent the problem. Then numbers were paired that added to ten (1 and 9, 2 and 8, 3 and 7, 4 and 6). There was also a row of 10 dots making 5 tens in all with another row of 5 dots.

Approach 3

Numbers from 1 to 10 were written in a column and consecutive pairs of numbers were added. Then those sums were added in pairs.

Approach 4

The first step was recording the sums for 1 + 2 and 3 + 4. Next, 3 and 7 were added. At that point the remaining numbers were added consecutively to the preceding sum using counting on to find each sum.

Approach 1

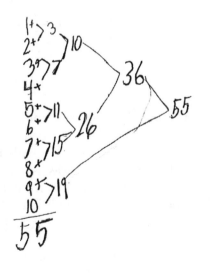

Approach 2

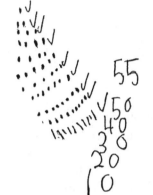

$1 + 9 = 10$

$2 + 8 = 10$

$3 + 7 = 10$

$4 + 6 = 10$

Approach 3

Approach 4

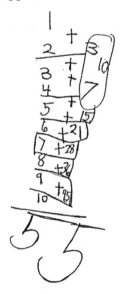

85

Vignette 1

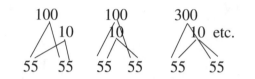

Kayla and Danny wrote 55 twenty times and thought of each number as 50 + 5. They began by pairing 2 fifties to make 100 and also wrote the sequence for counting by 100s (100, 200, 300, . . .). They then grouped 2 fives to get ten and counted by 10 to 100. Putting 1000 and 100 together gave them 1100.

Vignette 2

Danny	Tasha	Clint	Erica	etc.
50	50	50	50 . . .	
50	100	150	200 . . .	

After initially struggling, Valerie wrote each child's name with 50 beneath it. Then she wrote the sequence for counting by fifty. Finally, she wrote 20 fives and grouped them to make tens.

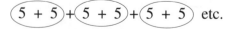

Note: another variation was to draw 20 squares (i.e., desks) and write 50 inside each one. The children used a calculator, but had trouble coordinating "button-pushing" with marking off the squares as they were counted.

Vignette 3

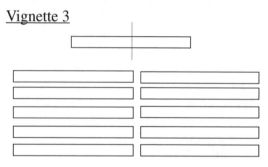

Maria and Denise used tens rods. To represent the number of dots needed for 2 people, they made 2 sets of 5 tens with an eleventh rod placed so that 5 was assigned to each group. They made 100s from the 50s; then they added in the additional 10 tens.

Vignette 4

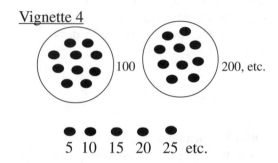

Aaron and Carlos used beans in two ways. First, each bean was assigned the value of 10. Thus each circle (see above) contained two sets of 50, or 100. Then beans were assigned a value of 5 and twenty beans were placed in a row to be counted by fives.

Vignette 5

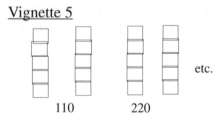

Adam and Andrew first used a calculator to compute 20 x 55. To check their work, they made 20 stacks of 5 cubes and arbitrarily assigned a value of 55 to each stack. They mentally added 55 and 55 to get 110 and counted by 110s to 1100.

Dealing with Basic Facts

This section directly addresses the building of children's computational strategies. It applies the ideas presented on pages 59 to 63 to an aspect of the curriculum that continues to be important to many teachers and parents.

While most individuals agree that it is important for students to "know basic facts," there is often great disagreement about how students learn basic facts. Statements like the ones below reflect the beliefs of many teachers and parents.

"The only way students learn facts is through extensive drill."

"Students can't do advanced mathematics if they don't know facts."

These statements *do not* reflect our beliefs. They remind us, however, that this area must be addressed in our work. Thus, we give careful attention to facts and monitor children's progress.

Fortunately, there is extensive research that gives us direction. We have learned, for example, that children learn and retain facts when this work is a long-term goal that is addressed in the context of overall program goals.

We also are guided by research that clearly indicates children's learning and retention is facilitated when they acquire mature strategies. Finally, when children believe that mathematics makes sense and that they can learn mathematics, concepts and skills that were once difficult for them become much easier.

Six key elements of our work are described in this section, followed by examples and teaching suggestions.

Most "fact" work occurs in the context of problems, routines, and tasks.

In our classrooms, work with facts is usually embedded in tasks such as solving problems, exploring patterns, and discussing strategies. That is, there is a reason for adding, subtracting, multiplying, or dividing numbers. Thus, we seldom work with facts for their own sake.

Many examples throughout this book illustrate this approach. In the example at right, children were finding the cost of three items purchased at a school store. Notice that the computation involves both basic facts and two-digit numbers.

Children's Thinking for $4¢ + 13¢ + 7¢$

"I took the 3 from the 13 and put it with the 7 to make ten. The 10 plus the 10 in 13 makes 20 . . . and 20 + 4 is 24."

"4 plus 3 equals 7. Add the other 7 and that's 14. Then 14 + 10 equals 24."

"I took 3 from the 4 (the student pointed to the 4¢) and added it to the 7 to make it a ten. Now I have 10 and 10 and 1 and 3. That makes 24."

Note: In the last example, the student thought of 4 as 3 and 1. She put 3 and 7 together to get 10. She also thought of 13 as 10 and 3.

Fact work is woven throughout the mathematics program.

Rather than being confined to "fact" chapters such as "Addition Facts to 10" or "Subtraction Facts to 18," work with basic facts is woven into the program throughout the year. We also do not devote two or three weeks early in the year just to facts.

This approach is consistent with our view that many children need an extended window of opportunity in order to learn. The ongoing emphasis also is a key factor in promoting memorization and retention.

Another aspect of this principle is that work with basic facts occurs together with understanding and computing with two- and three-digit numbers. In fact, we notice that computing with multi-digit numbers helps children see why they need to learn facts and appears to promote mature strategies.

Facts of all sizes and operations are integrated.

Children regularly work with many kinds of facts—both in terms of the operation and the "size" of the numbers or answer.

Thus, on the same day they may use and discuss 5 + 2, 7 + 9, and 10 - 8.

This also is very different from traditional practice. We don't develop "easy" facts before "harder" facts; we also don't work with addition facts exclusively before working with subtraction facts. The "Number of the Day" routine promotes working with more than one operation.

One advantage of an integrated approach is that children see the relationship between a fact and its use in mental computation. Not only do they see 8 + 2, but they also use it as they solve 48 + 2. Similarly they see a connection between 10 - 8 and 30 - 28.

Another advantage is that children have multiple opportunities to work with multiplication and division facts, topics that traditionally are not emphasized in primary programs. For example, a child might solve a problem involving 4 sixes by using doubles: "I doubled 6 to get 12 and then I doubled 12 to get 24." Shortly, some children will shift to the traditional language: "2 times 6 is 12 and 2 times 12 is 24."

Children also regularly solve division problems. They use what they know about 4 sixes, for example, to determine how 24 pennies can be shared among 4 children.

Children introduce strategies; teachers highlight these strategies by regularly reinforcing and referring to them.

Some characteristics of this approach:

- It builds on children's reasoning, rather than on our designing lessons around particular strategies.

- It views learning strategies as occurring over time rather than in a few days.

- It recognizes that there can be several different ways children think about a fact, rather than one preferred method. For example, some children recall 6 + 7 by using 6 + 6. Other children may take 3 from the 6 and put it with the 7 to make 10 and then add 10 and 3.

Most of the common fact strategies listed at right are suggested by the children. We find that children bring an awareness of strategies from previous experiences. At times, however, we suggest additional ways of thinking for children to consider. The main point is that we make sure that children develop mature thinking strategies.

Using strategies to learn facts is not new; there are sixty years of research on the role of strategies in promoting memorization. However, our work has shown us new ways to make their use more effective.

When we focus specifically on facts, most often we focus on children's thinking for a few facts, rather than finding answers for many facts.

This principle is consistent with the previous discussion and is a major factor in promoting mature thinking. These extended discussions also help children respond quickly and confidently through providing time and opportunities for learning efficient approaches. This is particularly valuable for less mature students.

Discussions occur in many ways. For example, to solve a problem, children needed to find how many wheels were needed to build 5 wagons. This led to an extended conversation about ways this might be done. In such situations, children learn that 5 fours is 20; they also learn ways of thinking about 5 fours.

A second example might occur during a daily math warm-up. The teacher presents three basic facts, such as 8 + 4, 12 - 5, and 11 - 9 and asks children to share how they would find the answers. This approach is basic for daily routines involving finding the sum of several numbers, which are described on pages 94 and 95.

Common Fact Strategies

Addition

Count On

Use Doubles

Group to Make Ten

Use a Known Fact

Subtraction

Count On

Count Back

Use Doubles

Use Ten

Use Addition

As a result, we seldom ask children to compute 25 facts and find only the answer. This is not as effective as having them practice both the strategies and the answer. Further, this approach is consistent with what we value in mathematics and what we want children to know and be able to do mathematically.

Short practice periods are used periodically to assess children's progress in recalling facts.

Children also need experiences that encourage them to become fluent with facts; that is, to respond reasonably quickly. However, this work needs to be carefully thought through in terms of its purpose, timing, and approach.

Our practice work tends to be brief, oral, and oriented toward individual growth. We also delay such work until children have a firm understanding of operations, effective strategies, and confidence in their thinking. Thus, practice periods occur later and less frequently than in traditional classrooms. While fluency with facts is important, we believe that is a *by-product* of children's work rather than the *direct goal* of it.

Ongoing practice can occur in many ways. Daily routines provide one avenue; the routine also includes an emphasis on using appropriate strategies.

A few facts can be woven into daily warm-ups or such moments as lining up for recess. We also use activities, including games, that encourage quick responses, while deemphasizing the competitive aspects. Asking children to identify facts they "just know" versus ones they have to "think about" also is useful.

We are careful not to put pressure on children or cause them to feel anxious. For that reason we avoid such common practices as "timed tests," as typically used. When all young children are required to meet an arbitrary standard at an arbitrary time, it frequently causes them to doubt their mathematical capabilities. We firmly believe that there are more appropriate and productive ways.

Children learn in their own ways and on their own schedules; we must respect this and communicate to children our confidence in their ability to learn.

Using Facts in Everyday Problems

As we have noted, fact work occurs in many ways. Early work with partitioning numbers (see pages 80 to 82), for example, certainly involves basic facts. In this section, additional ways that teachers address facts are provided.

Several examples of different types of addition and subtraction problems are described at right.[1] The primary focus of the work is problem solving; in using such problems, children's understanding of operations and the kinds of situations to which operations apply is broadened and strengthened.

At first glance, the problems don't cause one to think of learning facts. The discussion is placed here to emphasize that concept and skill work can complement each other and can be intertwined. For example, as children share their strategies for solving problems, they often share computational strategies for facts. Discussions for the first problem might involve counting on, counting back, doubles, use of a known fact, and so on.

[1] The Cognitively Guided Instruction project emphasizes the regular use of such problems. Articles by Bebout and Carpenter (1989) and Carpenter, Carey, and Kouba (1990) discuss the approach in detail.

The action in this problem is joining; children must find the unknown part.

1. *Maria has 5 crayons. How many more crayons does she need if she wants 11 crayons in call?*

The action of separating, and the part taken away is unknown.

3. *Mark had 11 crayons and gave some of them to Maria. He had 5 crayons left. How many crayons did he give to Maria?*

No action is indicated and children must find the unknown part.

5. *Maria has 11 crayons. Five are red and the rest are blue. How many blue crayons does she have?*

In this comparison problem, one quantity is unknown. The relationship between the two quantities is given.

7. *Maria has 5 crayons. Mark has 6 more than Maria. How many crayons does Mark have?*

In this joining problem, the initial part is unknown.

2. *Maria had some crayons. Then she found 5 more. Now she has 11 crayons. How many crayons did she start with?*

This is a separating problem in which the total amount is unknown.

4. *Maria had some crayons. She gave Mark 5 of them. She has 6 crayons left. How many crayons did she start with?*

This comparison states the two quantities. The difference between them is unknown.

6. *Maria has 11 crayons and Mark has 5 crayons. How many more crayons does Maria have than Mark?*

We have become increasingly aware of the importance of having discussions with children in which their strategies are the focus. Sometimes we have the children identify the strategies that were used and record them by name. Sometimes we discuss strategies that are efficient for a fact versus ones that might be inefficient. For 8 + 9, *using doubles* and *making ten* are efficient strategies, whereas counting on is not particularly efficient.

These discussions encourage *all* children to *think about thinking* and to be more aware of their own thinking, as well as that of others. In several cases it helped children who still needed to *count all* to move beyond that.

Attaching names to strategies is also important. Communication is facilitated when an idea can be expressed using a label that has meaning to everyone and enhances discourse. Thus, names are a means, not an end in themselves.

What We Know About Addition

You have some things and you get more.

If you add 0 to any number, the answer is the same number.

Doubles are good to know.

$$3 + 3 = 6 \quad 6 + 6 = 12$$

Doubles plus one helps you know facts.

$4 + 5 = 9$ because	$7 + 8 = 15$ because
$4 + 4 = 8$ and $8 + 1 = 9$	$7 + 7 = 14$ and $14 + 1 = 15$

If you add 1 to any number, the answer is always the next number you count.

When you add 9 to a number, your answer is one less than the number you added plus 10.

$$9 + \underline{5} = 1\underline{4} \quad 9 + \underline{3} = 1\underline{2}$$

You can count on to find answers.

$$8 + 2 \quad 8 \ldots 9, 10$$

What We Know About Subtraction

To subtract, think of the other part.

$6 - 2 = \underline{?}$
Think: $2 + \underline{4} = 6$

When you count back, don't count the number you're starting with or you'll be one off.

$8 - 3 = 5$
$8 \ldots \underline{7}, 6, 5,$

Counting back works best when the numbers are far apart.

$11 - 2 = ?$
$11 \ldots 10, 9$

Counting up works well when you have two numbers that are close together.

$20 - 18$
$18 \ldots 19, 20$

If you have a number and you subtract that same number, the answer is always 0.

$1001 - 1001 = 0$

When you subtract neighbors, the answer is 1.

$8 - 7 = 1$
$14 - 13 = 1$

15 - 5 = 10, so if it is 15 - 6, you take one away from 10 and get 9.

$$\begin{array}{r} 15 \\ -\ 6 \\ \hline 9 \end{array} \qquad \begin{array}{r} 14 \\ -\ 5 \\ \hline 9 \end{array}$$

Look for part of a double.

$12 - 6 = \underline{6}$

One helpful technique for introducing summary discussions about strategies themselves is to ask children what they know about addition and subtraction. Two examples of ideas shared by the children are presented on these pages. Teachers typically record the children's suggestions, thus building a class list that is posted for ongoing reference and refinement.

The children's contributions remind us that they bring much informal knowledge to the classroom. Some of this knowledge has been acquired in nonschool settings. The knowledge we gain provides additional insights into how children think and what they know, and thus forms the basis for our work.

Learning Facts Through Daily Routines

As noted earlier, daily routines can have an important role in promoting learning. Several involve facts and provide opportunity for children to practice facts and strategies in an engaging way. All of them cause students to use mature strategies and develop fluency.

Pockets Routine. One first grade teacher captured the dynamics of a routine that emerged from a part-whole activity. Students find the number of pockets in their shirt, their pants, and then in all. She writes:

"My children have really been enjoying the pockets activity. For them, though, the favorite part was finding how many pockets for the entire class. The first day we had 85 pockets, and now we're up to 122. Now it doesn't matter to them if their clothes match in the morning; it's whether they have a lot of pockets!

"We first find the total for each small group, such as: 2 + 5 + 4 + 4 + 5 + 5. One group began with the 3 fives and counted by 5s to 15. Other groups found different ways of making the task manageable and, as a result, to move beyond counting by ones. (Continued on next page.)

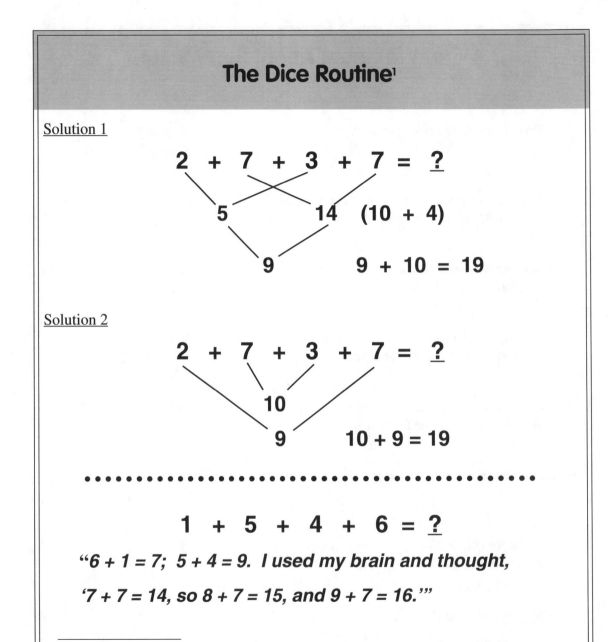

The Dice Routine[1]

<u>Solution 1</u>

$$2 + 7 + 3 + 7 = \underline{?}$$

5   14   (10 + 4)

9   9 + 10 = 19

<u>Solution 2</u>

$$2 + 7 + 3 + 7 = \underline{?}$$

10

9   10 + 9 = 19

• •

$$1 + 5 + 4 + 6 = \underline{?}$$

"6 + 1 = 7; 5 + 4 = 9. I used my brain and thought, '7 + 7 = 14, so 8 + 7 = 15, and 9 + 7 = 16.'"

---

[1] A number cube is rolled 4 times. The numbers are recorded and children are asked to find the total. After children think individually for a few moments, various ways of thinking are shared.

Daily Oral Language Routine[1]

4 + 9 + 7 + 6

9 plus 7 equals 16.
Take the 6 in 16.
4 + 6 = 10
10 plus 10 plus
6 equals 26.

4 + 6 equals 10.
Change 9 + 7 to 10 + 6.
10 plus 10 equals 20.
20 plus 6 equals 26.

7 minus 1 equals 6.
1 + 9 equals 10.
6 plus 6 equals 12.
10 + 12 equals 22.
22 plus 4 equals 26.

9 plus 7 equals 16.
16 plus 4 equals 20.
20 plus 6 equals 26.

7 plus 4 equals 11.
6 plus 9 equals 15.
10 plus 10 equals 20.
20 plus 6 equals 26.

Take 1 from the 7.
6 and 6 is 12.
1 and 9 is 10.
12 and 10 is 22.
22 and 4 is 26.

---

[1] The numbers are generated from the errors in each of 4 sentences. After correcting, children find the total number of errors. The following sentence has 4 errors: *the boys catched the fotball*

<u>Dice Routine</u>. Page 94 shows a second successful and motivating routine. Here, first graders are finding the sum of four numbers generated by rolling a die. Over time, they became adept at breaking numbers apart and combining them in multiple ways. The use of "chunking" notation facilitated their thinking.

<u>Daily Oral Language Routine</u>. In a second grade classroom (see left), a daily oral language routine involved correcting errors in spelling, punctuation and grammar for 4 sentences. Each day the children found the total number of errors by adding the errors for each sentence. The teacher had several children share their thinking. In each of these routines, having multiple addends encouraged mature strategies.

Children anticipate these routines and are often disappointed when they are omitted. Over time, strategies become more complex as children explore new approaches. Teachers then ask children to classify strategies as "fun" or "efficient" to help children reflect on their thinking.

Using Tools: Base-Ten Blocks and Hundreds Charts

Introduction

Many tools, including counters, money, and drawings, provide support for children's computational reasoning; particularly in early stages of work. Recently, we particularly have been impressed with the contribution of base-ten blocks and hundreds charts throughout the year. Both promote deeper understanding and efficient computational strategies and are helpful when computing with two- and three-digit numbers.

Rationale

More specifically, these tools

- broaden the range of children's strategies,

- contributes to children's number sense,

- promote mature ways of thinking,

- provide visual support for mental strategies,

- highlight tens and ones ideas in computation, and

- provide additional ways of validating mental and written solutions.

Guidelines

Our use of hundreds charts and base-ten blocks has evolved over the past three years. The following points capture key aspects of our experience:

- The materials are introduced early in the year and used throughout the year. Initial exploratory experiences introduce the materials. Later there may be short blocks of time when the materials and connections are made to computation. This approach provides extended time for children to become familiar with each tool and to understand the related mathematics.

This contrasts with our initial approach in which each tool was "taught" in a miniunit at specific times during the year. "Teaching the tool" led to prescribed ways of using it, which tended to obscure the mathematics involved. Weaving the tools throughout the program has reduced problems in understanding and using them insightfully, as there is now an expanded window of opportunity to learn.

- We let children use the tools in ways that make sense to them rather than requiring using them in prescribed ways. Many of us remember, for example, the frustrations of trying to get children to use base-ten blocks to parallel the steps of the traditional paper-and-pencil algorithm.

- Children select the tool that makes sense to them. Some children, for example, make regular and frequent use of the hundreds chart, while others find the base-ten blocks most helpful.

- Opportunities for all children to reflect on the use of these tools occurs during the seminars when children share their strategies. While the children are working we observe which children use these tools and ask them to share their strategy. During their presentation we emphasize the mathematics ideas and approach; at times, we have all children try the approach.

The two examples at right were among the strategies selected by the students in the class to solve a problem.

The next several pages provide examples of how we introduce and use each tool.

Mom reads 15 minutes to her children every night except Saturday and Sunday. How many minutes does she read to them a week?

Both the hundreds-chart and the base-ten blocks provided a way of representing the above problem, as well as a way of finding the answer. The children using the hundreds chart thought, "I went down 10 (1 row) and counted over 5 each time."

It is interesting that the children who used the base-ten blocks used only the tens rods. To show 5 ones, they used a tens rod and covered the top half of it.

Introducing the Hundreds Chart

Many teachers introduce the hundreds chart through daily routines; these early experiences help children understand

- that numbers are not arranged in the same way as on the number line or some gameboards;

1	2	3	4	5	6	7	8	9	10
								12	11

- how to move to the next number when reaching the end of a row. For example, when counting from 20 to 21 you need to move to the left end of the next row; and

- the ten more/ten less relationship between numbers in a column. On the number line, 15 is ten units to the right of 5. On the hundreds chart it is below 5;

1	2	3	4	5	6	7	8	9	10
11	12	13	14	15	16	17	18		

Recording the Number of Days in School

```
  +---+---+---+---+---+
 25  26  [27] 28  29  30
```

1	2	3	4	5	6	7	8	9	10
11	12	13	14	15	16	17	18	19	20
21	22	23	24	25	26	27			

In many first and second grade classrooms, children show the number of days they have been in school on both a number line and a hundreds chart. This allows children to construct the hundreds chart one day at a time. These daily experiences provide ongoing opportunities to explore the many number patterns that can be highlighted on the hundreds chart.

Constructing the Hundreds Chart

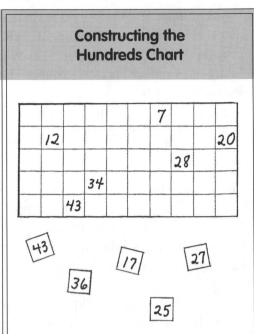

The above activity can be used to introduce the hundreds chart. After a card (i.e., 27) is selected, the children represent the number using connecting cubes grouped by tens. They are laid on the chart so that they cover two rows of ten and 7 more squares. After discussing that the "last" square covered by the blocks represents 27, the card is placed on the chart.

A few numbers can be "added" each day. Patterns that the children notice can be discussed.

See Burns 1994.

Moving about the Hundreds Chart

Children's understanding of the arrangement of numbers can be assessed by their facility in moving quickly and confidently on the hundreds chart.

It is particularly important for students to be able to count by tens starting with any number by moving up or down a column. This is particularly important for adding and subtracting two-digit numbers.

Some children need considerable time and multiple experiences before they develop this understanding. Even when shown the "shortcut," they continue to count by ones, making the strategy their own only when it makes sense to them.

Activities that provide children opportunities to explore "moving on the hundreds chart" help them develop mature and productive strategies.

Spinning and Moving

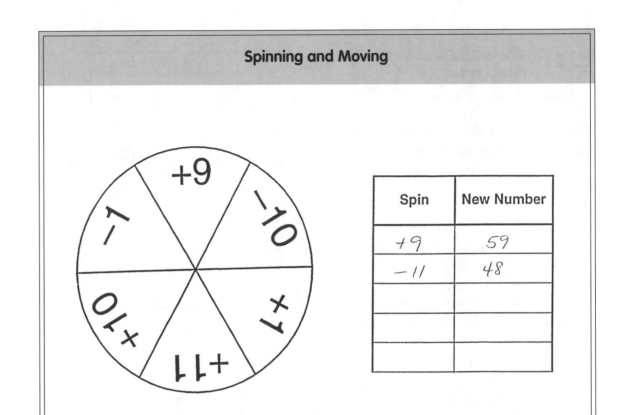

Spin	New Number
+9	59
−11	48

A spinner game can help children learn ways of moving about the hundred chart. The game begins with the markers at 50 on the hundreds chart. Children take turns spinning and moving their markers. The goal can be "being ahead" after 10 moves or reaching a target number, such as 100. Initially, the children may just spin and move. Later, it can be useful to have them record their moves.

The activity can be used to assess the ways the children are thinking. Over time, they move from counting by ones to using shortcuts, which they learn from one another. Some children go beyond the "tens" shortcut to create strategies for adding and subtracting 9 and 11.

Adapted from *Math Trailblazers*, Grade 1, Unit 9, 1997

Computing on the Hundreds Chart

Some children make the hundreds chart their primary computational tool for an extended period. Their strategies provide new ways of thinking.

One strategy is adding or subtracting "in parts" from a starting number. For example, it is natural on the hundreds chart to solve 48 + 23 by starting with 48, adding 20 and then adding 3 (Example 1). Similarly, for 52 - 24, one can subtract 20 and then 4 (Example 2).

The hundreds chart also leads to mental shortcuts for adding numbers close to a multiple of ten. For 48 + 19, one can add 20 to 48 and then subtract 1 from 68 (Example 3).

Children also use the chart for finding the difference between numbers, such as 74 and 100. One approach is to count by tens and then by ones (Example 4).

Finally, children generalize such patterns as 8 + 2, 28 + 2, 68 + 2 and 10 - 2, 30 - 2, 50 - 2.

Example 1: 48 + 23

48...58...68...69...70...71

Example 2: 52 - 24

52...42...32...31...30...29...28

Example 3: 48 + 19

48...58...68...67

Example 4: 74 + ? = 100

74...84...94...95...96...97...98...99...100

The Two-Hundreds Chart

It is special when the two-hundreds chart is introduced, for children begin to feel truly powerful in working with numbers.

No longer are they restricted to 65 + 23, but can now compute 165 + 23. Children can now add two-digit numbers whose sum is greater than 100. They can also compute 150 - 27 or 162 - 138.

Children often choose to extend their computational work beyond the two-hundreds chart. For 165 + 128, they first add 165 and 28 and then add 100 to the answer. Some children create three-hundreds charts by extending the two-hundreds charts and create such computational problems as 265 - 128 to solve. A variety of advanced strategies often emerge; sometimes children try to solve the same problem in more than one way.

It is evident that some children are truly having mathematical fun as they "mess with numbers" in various ways.

1	2	3	4	5	6	7	8	9	10
11	12	13	14	15	16	17	18	19	20
21	22	23	24	25	26	27	28	29	30
31	32	33	34	35	36	37	38	39	40
41	42	43	44	45	46	47	48	49	50
51	52	53	54	55	56	57	58	59	60
61	62	63	64	65	66	67	68	69	70
71	72	73	74	75	76	77	78	79	80
81	82	83	84	85	86	87	88	89	90
91	92	93	94	95	96	97	98	99	100
101	102	103	104	105	106	107	108	109	110
111	112	113	114	115	116	117	118	119	120
121	122	123	124	125	126	127	128	129	130
131	132	133	134	135	136	137	138	139	140
141	142	143	144	145	146	147	148	149	150
151	152	153	154	155	156	157	158	159	160
161	162	163	164	165	166	167	168	169	170
171	172	173	174	175	176	177	178	179	180
181	182	183	184	185	186	187	188	189	190
191	192	193	194	195	196	197	198	199	200

Transitions to Base-Ten Blocks

Children's work with groups of tens and ones grows out of their experiences in finding the number of objects by grouping them and then counting the number of groups and the number left over.

We plan many experiences in which children group by twos, fives, and tens and then count accordingly to find the number of objects.

The grouping might occur by placing 10 objects in plastic bags, filling tens frames, or making stacks of 10 connecting cubes. Forming stacks of cubes eventually leads to the use of base-ten blocks. The cubes can be counted several ways:

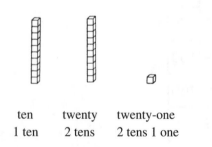

| ten | twenty | twenty-one |
| 1 ten | 2 tens | 2 tens 1 one |

These kinds of experiences promote insightful use of base-ten blocks.

Number of Letters: An Initial Grouping Experience

Form groups of 4 or 5 children. Have each child make a train of cubes showing the number of letters in his or her first name.

Next, the number of letters in each group is found by combining individual trains and making as many stacks of ten cubes as possible. The blocks from each group are placed on the chalkrail for comparison and discussion (see below).

To find the number of letters in everyone's name for the entire class, the cubes are regrouped to make as many additional stacks of ten as possible. The children count by tens and then by ones to find the total.

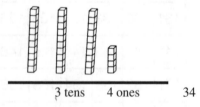

3 tens   4 ones   34

As an extension, have the children repeat the activity, this time using the number of letters in the children's last names.

Using Base-Ten Blocks in Computation

Children use stacks of tens and ones or base-ten blocks throughout Grades 1 and 2 in many ways. It is also important to connect this work to solving problems and doing computation.

Often, there are children who choose base-ten blocks to help them solve problems. Whenever this occurs, teachers have these children explain their work. This helps all children become familiar with using the blocks as a computational tool.

If children use the blocks, teachers may ask a volunteer to show how the blocks might be used to verify a particular strategy.

Another approach is to devote one or two days to having all children use the blocks to solve computational problems. This helps children have more options, and profit from their classmates' explanations about their use of the blocks.

A Whole-Class Investigation in Computing with Base-Ten Blocks

Give each pair or small group of children a tub of base-ten blocks and have them represent several two- and three-digit numbers.

Then give them a few problems to solve using the blocks, such as the ones below. Observe their work and have the children present their methods to the whole class for discussion.

$$17 - 9$$
$$67 + 24$$
$$112 - 30$$

In one classroom, two methods for solving 17 - 9 were shared. Both students started with 1 ten and 7 ones (see below). One child removed 7 blocks and then covered 2 units on the tens rod with his fingers. The second child said, "I removed a tens rod. And then threw one cube back in because I was only supposed to subtract 9."

Computing with Base-Ten Blocks

Adding and subtracting larger numbers involves working with tens and ones and the idea that 1 ten is equivalent to 10 ones.

Although children use their own strategies for using the blocks, they are dealing with key grouping and place value ideas related to the traditional algorithm. Teacher-led discussions highlight children's reasoning with tens and ones and the connection between 1 ten and 10 ones.

When adding, children tend to begin with the tens rods, and work from left to right. When subtracting, children typically do not replace a tens rod with 10 ones, but rather use the "cover-up" method shown at the right or the "throw-back" method mentioned on page 103.

As these ideas are revisited over time, children become conversant with the concepts and more flexible in their thinking about tens and ones.

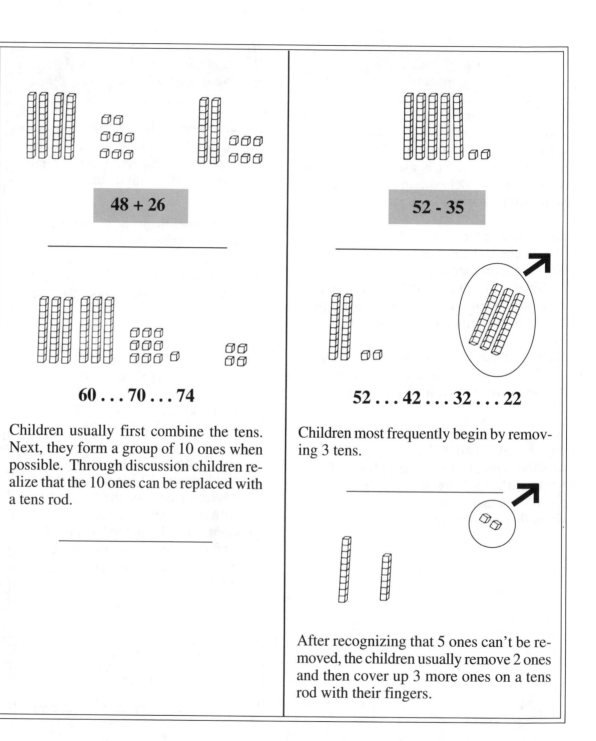

48 + 26

60 . . . 70 . . . 74

Children usually first combine the tens. Next, they form a group of 10 ones when possible. Through discussion children realize that the 10 ones can be replaced with a tens rod.

52 - 35

52 . . . 42 . . . 32 . . . 22

Children most frequently begin by removing 3 tens.

After recognizing that 5 ones can't be removed, the children usually remove 2 ones and then cover up 3 more ones on a tens rod with their fingers.

The base-ten blocks make it easy for children to compute with three-digit numbers. The children enjoy creating and solving these problems, since the work causes them to feel mathematically powerful. As noted earlier, they consider this mathematical "play."

Three-digit computation extends their grouping and place value knowledge. They see, for example, that 1 hundred is the same as 10 tens or even 9 tens and 10 ones. They also connect adding 3 and 4 and adding 3 tens and 4 tens.

A problem involving 112 - 30 can lead to a discussion that 110 is also 11 tens (see the top example). One child then explained that any three-digit number can be read as a number of tens. For example, 200 is 20 tens and 215 is 21 tens and 5 ones.

The second example illustrates the use of the blocks to add 365 and 157. Sometimes, 10 tens are traded for 1 hundred, although they may be left as 10 tens.

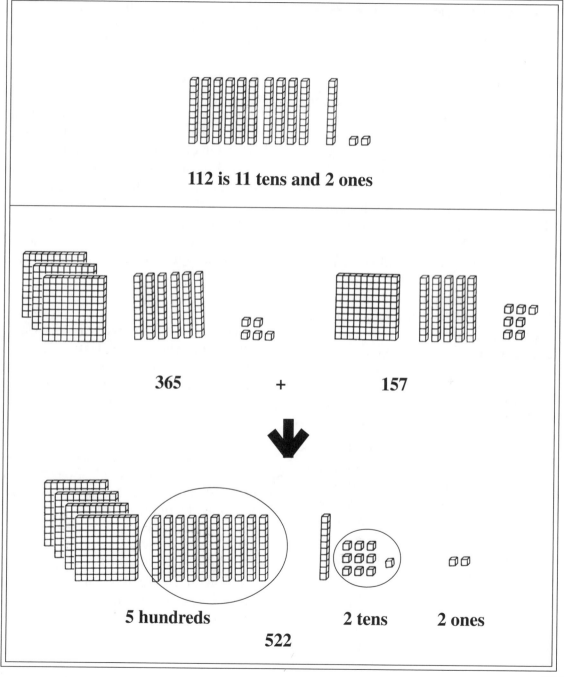

112 is 11 tens and 2 ones

365 + **157**

5 hundreds **2 tens** **2 ones**

522

Developing Standard Algorithms

The Context

Instruction on standard algorithms occurs in Grade 2. It also occurs in a *very different context* with our students for they have had a *very different mathematical experience* than the typical one. These children have developed strong number sense and many computational strategies. (Pages 58 to 62 present the overall approach and page 54 discusses standard algorithms.)

On many occasions, the children have discussed standard algorithms during class seminars. Thus, they know about standard algorithms and have some sense of how they work. A few children use them regularly as one of their approaches.

When the Work Occurs

Generally, the algorithms receive direct attention in March or April, or whenever the teacher feels this work would be appropriate. Thus, the time this instruction occurs varies from classroom to classroom and from year to year. We have learned that *when* this is taught is *not* as important as *what knowledge* the students have when this is developed.

Teachers use their insights about their students' development to decide when to begin. The teachers assess such factors as children's thinking, their understanding of underlying ideas, and their fluency with oral and written invented algorithms.

How It Is Done

The work can be launched in several ways. The teacher might highlight a child's presentation of a standard algorithm and ask follow-up questions. Alternatively, she might present the standard algorithm, indicating that this is a method she has seen others use, and challenge the children to make sense of the procedure. A students' comment might be the impetus for analyzing the algorithm.

Once the task is presented, the work proceeds similarly to other lessons: time is provided for children to work together, various materials are available, and there is an extended discussion.

The children might check their work using an invented procedure. They also might demonstrate how the base-ten blocks show how the algorithm works. The children then could work in pairs on a second example, followed by a class discussion. To conclude, children use the standard algorithm for a few additional practice exercises. The work continues in much the same manner with a few practice exercises each day.

$$38 + 26$$

$$30 + 20 = 50$$
$$8 + 6 = 14$$
$$50 + 10 = 60$$
$$60 + 4 = 64$$

Written forms of invented procedures often highlight the same place value ideas on which traditional algorithms are based. Thus, initial work with nonstandard algorithms provides the underpinnings for a smooth transition to standard algorithms.

Extra attention is provided to complexities inherent in the subtraction algorithm. For example, in 42 - 15, some children think 5 - 2 when subtracting the ones, rather than realizing that 2 - 5 is not possible.

We notice several differences in our current work with standard algorithms as compared to past experiences. Now children move easily from addition to subtraction, often dealing with both algorithms within the same set of lessons. Far less instructional time and far less practice is needed.

The way base-ten blocks are used is another difference. In the past, we began with the blocks and directed children's use of them in a step-by-step manner. As a result, the children learned both a "block" algorithm and a paper-and-pencil algorithm. The lessons often did not proceed smoothly; additionally, both we and the children often were frustrated.

Our children have a strong, connected, and flexible understanding of grouping and place value ideas from their extensive experience with them. As a result, the role of base-ten blocks is to (1) support children's reasoning, and (2) clarify the mathematical ideas of the algorithms. They now are used in a more informal and student-directed manner.

As we reflect on the work, we are delighted with how much better the results are today than in the past. Not only does the work proceed smoothly, but children find it easy and even enjoy it.

Maintaining a Broad Computational Perspective

Standard algorithms are useful ways of computing; this is also true of mental and other invented algorithms. We want our children to use many strategies. Thus, the acquisition of traditional paper-and-pencil algorithms is not the end goal, but merely one of many computational goals.

We continue to pose and discuss many kinds of problems. Many times, invented procedures are easier and more natural than standard algorithms. We notice that most children use their own strategies regularly, along with standard algorithms. They seem to enjoy creating and using their own strategies.

We also discuss when it might be easier to compute mentally as compared to computing with standard or other written algorithms. Occasionally, we ask the class to list examples that might fit each type of computation. Some of their suggestions are shown at right.

Simpler "In Our Heads"

100 - 5	*25 + 25*
37 + 19	*28 + 32*
50 - 13	*70 - 35*
80 - 75	*66 - 7*

Simpler with Paper and Pencil

86 + 48	*38 + 16 + 47*
17 + 76	*84 - 37*
65 - 38	*116 - 79*

Some children enjoy extending their work with standard algorithms to three- and four-digit numbers. This leads to new understandings about place value and renaming numbers. These investigations are driven by the students' curiosity about numbers.

We remind ourselves frequently of the importance of developing computation within the context of developing children's number sense and mathematical reasoning. It has been satisfying to us that standard algorithms can be taught in this context while maintaining a balance among the various ways of computing. Our students find that standard algorithms are useful tools, while continuing to examine alternative computational strategies that promote mathematical growth.

The following two vignettes describe the experiences of two second grade teachers as their children broadened their knowledge of addition and subtraction strategies to include standard algorithms.

From the Classroom

$$
\begin{array}{r}
3\,6 \\
+\,4\,8 \\
\hline
1\,4 \\
+\,7\,0 \\
\hline
8\,4
\end{array}
\qquad
\begin{array}{l}
6 + 8 = 14 \\
30 + 40 = 70
\end{array}
$$

Over time, my second grade inner-city students had become comfortable with the above strategy that they developed for adding two-digit numbers. Their strategy grew out of their place value knowledge and ways of "breaking numbers apart."

Whenever we did an addition problem I asked, "Does anyone have another way to solve it?" One day, I thought that renaming would emerge from a class discussion. Merritt had introduced his concept of a "magic number," referring to the "1" that is often written above the tens column. Although he sensed there was a place where the "magic 1" should go, he could not explain his thinking further and I decided not to pursue the discussion further at this time.

Old concerns about learning the traditional algorithms began to surface in January, including student performance on the upcoming standardized test and the expectations of third grade teachers.

After discussing my concerns with project leaders, I decided to let my students continue to use their own methods, realizing that eventually they would see the connection of their work to the standard algorithm. I continued to ask, "Does anyone have another way to solve this?"

Several weeks later, Jenna, a student who doesn't take many risks, said we could make it easier and quicker by "adding the number once." I asked her to show us what she was thinking.

$$
\begin{array}{r}
1 \\
3\,6 \\
+\,4\,8 \\
\hline
8\,4
\end{array}
$$

She explained that we could just make a mark in the tens column or, if we could remember, to just hold it in our heads. Merritt observed that it was like the magic number he had talked about earlier.

Several students indicated they would like to try using Jenna's method. By the end of the lesson, most students understood Jenna's algorithm. Other students continued to use their old way of recording the work. I was comfortable with their decision, for I have learned that when students make sense of numbers and are ready to make the transition, they will let me know. The timing is their decision, not mine.

Marla Wehrle,
McKinstry Elementary School

From the Classroom

Although I have been teaching second grade for many years, I continue to be amazed at how children think and how involved they are in their learning. Throughout the year the children had been creating their own strategies for adding and subtracting and we had not worked with the standard written algorithms.

This would soon change on a February day—as a result of Sarah's dilemma with one problem. This led to all children learning the standard algorithm for subtraction in one day and being enthusiastic about their accomplishment.

The problem involved the amount of change from 50¢ if a 12¢ item was purchased. Many children wrote 50 - 10 = 40 and 40 - 2 = 38. Some subtracted 2 from 50 and then subtracted 10. As usual, I was really proud of their thinking.

The children were ready to leave, but Sarah still was holding her paper. She had written 50 - 12 vertically. She looked at me and said, "I know I can't take zero minus two, but I don't know what to do!" As she left she said, "I'm going to ask my dad how to do this tonight."

The next morning she was beaming and announced, "I know how to do it!" She showed me what her dad had taught her and she was so proud of herself. Normally, she is a reluctant student, so, I asked her if she would show her classmates her new way.

Sarah confidently went to the board with her piece of paper and explained that since she couldn't do zero minus two, she needed to get a ten. To get the 10, she crossed out the 5 (in 50) and wrote a 4; the 0 became a 10. Then she subtracted. She then did another problem her dad had given her. Soon a classmate said, "Oh, I know how to do it," and went to the board to work a problem as Sarah coached her. As more children said "I know how to do it," the process continued: one student would go to the board and another became the coach. The whole class was gradually included.

To challenge them, I wrote a problem that did not involve regrouping. Lisa immediately saw what to do, so she showed that if you don't have to regroup then just go ahead and subtract. As more children caught on, they helped the others.

I then had them do a few more subtraction problems. The children continued to work in pairs with one person writing and the other coaching. *They* decided who would be the writer and who would be the coach. The teaming gave more time to children who weren't ready to do the problem on their own. When they were ready to try, they had a partner to coach them if they needed it. This worked really, really well. I was delighted as we had accomplished a tremendous amount in 45 minutes. All children seemed fairly confident in renaming and also in knowing when to rename.

The next day Nathan said he had tried some addition problems at home. He figured if we could regroup in subtraction, there must be a way to do it with addition. He solved 64 + 28. First he said that 4 + 8 is 12; next he explained that since 12 had a ten in it, he could cross out the 6 in 64 and write a 7 above it. And then he added 7 tens and 2 tens. Finally, he shared two more problems that he had written down. A classmate said, "I know what you're doing" and as one child wrote, another one coached, as we had previously done.

A class discussion evolved when one team wrote the 12 as the ones total so the answer looked like 812 rather than 92. The children knew this was incorrect and that they needed to record the 1 ten differently. At that point I showed them that you could record a 1 above the tens column. Some children adopted this procedure and others continued to use Nathan's method. Some made use of a coach and some worked alone.

What an amazing experience! In two days my students had become very comfortable with standard addition and subtraction algorithms. In the past I had taught separate units on these algorithms and had worked and worked and worked and drilled and drilled and drilled.

This year was certainly different. I think one reason was that this work emerged when the children were ready to learn it. In the past I had decided when to work on standard algorithms. Now *they* determined the timing. When the standard algorithm emerged naturally, they seemed more open to it and it evolved in a much more relaxed atmosphere. It is coming from one of them and I think whenever one of their own peers introduces something they think, "Oh, (s)he can do it; so I can do it too."

Our work throughout the year on having children invent their own computational strategies for solving problems caused them to discover many ways of adding and subtracting. And since they had worked with the subtraction algorithm first, it seemed to Nathan to increase the tens digit by 1. He and others just applied what they already knew about subtraction. Their background in subtraction enabled them to create a slightly different addition algorithm.

Like many teachers, I worry that I won't cover important content if I don't intro-duce it. I also worry about what the teacher next year might say. As a result, my past tendency was to rush things and introduce content rather than being patient and letting students' work guide me.

One of the nicest aspects of my new approach is wondering what will happen next. I wonder what problems are going to be proposed in class tomorrow and I wonder which children will extend their work to larger numbers. I also enjoy having students tell me they can't wait until the next math class. I know all of us, including the teacher, is looking forward to that next day of new problems.

Melita Meyers,
St. Joseph's School

Appendix

"It sounds good, but does it really work?"
"How do I get other teachers to see that this is important?"
"What evidence is there that supports this approach?"

These are natural questions as we struggle with issues of making change. We often need reassurance; we also need to answer the questions of colleagues, administrators, and parents.

In recent years a number of researchers have turned their attention to learning in classrooms that emphasize learning through problems and making sense of mathematics. Several of these researchers are members of large-scale, multi-year projects which has permitted the study of variables and relationships over time. Several of the studies focus on student achievement with arithmetic concepts and skills.

This section highlights some of the studies that deal with problem-centered learning and developing understanding, as well as the relationship between understanding and skill. The brief annotations highlight key findings. If you need more details or further support, you might read the reports and share them with others. The references cited in the reports will help you find related literature and research.

• Carpenter, T. P., E. Ansell, M. L. Franke, E. Fennema, and L. Weisbeck. 1993. "Models of Problem Solving: A Study of Kindergarten Children's Problem-Solving Processes." *Journal for Research in Mathematics Education*, 24 (5): 428–441.

> The problem-solving performance of 70 kindergarten children who had solved single and multistep problems involving all four operations throughout the year is reported. A high level of performance on an interview was shown, with about half the chil-

dren using a valid strategy for all problems; almost two thirds of them correctly solved at least 7 of 9 problems. The authors note: "this study provides an existence proof that many kindergarten children can learn to solve problems . . . and they can apply this ability to a reasonably broad range of problems.

• Carpenter, T. P., M. L. Franke, V. R. Jacobs, E. Fennema, and S. B. Empson. 1997. "A Longitudinal Study of Invention and Understanding in Children's Multidigit Addition and Subtraction." *Journal for Research in Mathematics Education*, 29 (1): 3–20.

The role of invented strategies in developing multidigit addition and subtraction concepts and skills was the focus of this longitudinal study of 82 children from grades 1–3. Five interviews over three years focused on base-ten concepts, strategies for word problems, use of invented strategies, and flexibly using procedures. The researchers found that about 90% of children used invented strategies; they also concluded that "students who used invented strategies before they learned standard algorithms demonstrated better knowledge of base-ten number concepts and were more successful in extending their knowledge to new situations than were students who initially learned standard algorithms."

• Carraher, T. N., D. W. Carraher, and A. D. Schliemann. 1987. "Written and Oral Mathematics." *Journal for Research in Mathematics Education*, 18 (2): 83–97.

Fifteen third-grade Brazilian children were presented problems in three settings (simulated store, word problems, and computation exercises). Data show that children were far more likely to use oral methods in concrete situations and written school-learned algorithms for computation exercises. Children were also far more successful with oral than written methods. There were two types of oral strategies, decomposition (breaking quantities apart) and repeated grouping. Oral methods, which were learned in everyday settings rather than school, involved insightful ways of working with numbers. Examples are provided.

• Fennema, E., T. P. Carpenter, M. L. Franke, L. Levi, V. R. Jacobs, and S. B. Empson. 1996. "A Longitudinal Study of Learning to Use Children's Thinking in Mathematics Instruction." *Journal for Research in Mathematics Education*, 27 (4): 403–434.

Over 4 years the beliefs and instructional practices of 21 CGI primary teachers were studied. One major finding was that there were fundamental changes in the beliefs and teaching practices of 18 teachers, from demonstrating procedures to helping children build their mathematical thinking through solving problems and discussing their thinking. A second major finding was that there was a relationship between teacher change and students' achievement. In all cases, class concept and problem solving performance increased during the 4 years; there was no overall change in computation despite a shift in emphasis.

• Franke, M. L., and D. A. Carey. 1997. "Young Children's Perceptions of Mathematics in Problem-Solving Environments." *Journal for Research in Mathematics Education*, 28 (1): 8–25.

The study analyzes first-graders' perceptions of what it means to do mathematics in problem-solving classrooms. Thirty-six children from two different school systems were interviewed. Questions focused on what it means to do mathematics, what it means to solve a problem, use of a variety of approaches, and other variables. The researchers conclude, "Generally, the children perceived of mathematics as a problem-solving endeavor in which many different strategies are considered viable and communicating mathematical thinking is an integral part of the task."

• Hiebert, J., T. P. Carpenter, E. Fennema, K. C. Fuson, D. Wearne, H. Murray, A. Olivier, and P. Human. 1997. *Making Sense: Teaching and Learning Mathematics with Understanding*. Portsmouth, NH: Heinemann.

Although this powerful book is not a research study, it is the result of the five-year collaboration of researchers representing four projects. Each project has looked carefully at learning with understanding from a research and program development perspective. The central foci of the book are the essential features of classrooms, based on their research and observations, that promote mathematics understanding. These are the nature of classroom tasks, the role of the teacher, the social culture of the classroom, mathematical tools as learning supports, and equity and accessibility. A separate chapter captures the essence of classrooms in each project.

• Resnick, L. B., V. L. Bill, S. B. Lesgold, and M. N. Leer. 1991. "Thinking in Arithmetic Class." In *Teaching Advanced Skills to At-Risk Students: Views from Research and Practice*, ed. B. Means, C. Chelemer, and M. S. Knapp, 27–53. San Francisco: Jossey-Bass.

Included in this article is a report of a two-year problem-centered program stressing understanding in an inner-city school. One first grade and one second grade were involved. Six key principles of the program are presented. Data on a standardized mathematics test shows dramatic increase during the year, from the 25th to the 80th percentile in grade 1 and from the 30th to the 70th percentile in grade 2. Scores continued strong the following year. Highly positive results are described for three interviews during the year and anecdotal evidence is included about the children's confidence and attitudes.

• Thornton, C. A. and P. J. Smith. 1988. "Action Research: Strategies for Learning Subtraction Facts." *Arithmetic Teacher*, 35 (8): 8–13.

This research is representative of many studies that have examined the effects of incorporating thinking strategies into the learning of basic facts. First grade children whose instruction emphasized strategies significantly outperformed children receiving traditional instruction. The "strategies" group had a far greater mastery of addition and subtraction facts. They also had developed mature strategies to assist them in recalling facts. In a final interview, approximately 70 percent of the time the strategies group responded at an automatic level as compared to 44 percent of the traditional group.

• Villaseñor, Jr., A. and H. Kepner, Jr. 1993. "Arithmetic from a Problem-Solving Perspective: An Urban Implementation." *Journal of Research in Mathematics Education*, 24 (1): 62–69.

The performance of 12 classes of urban children whose teachers implemented a Cognitively Guided Instruction (CGI) approach, was compared with that of 12 control classrooms that used a traditional approach. The CGI students solved everyday problems on a regular basis with an emphasis on explaining one's thinking and discussing strategies. There was a significant (and substantial) difference favoring the CGI groups on a written problem-solving posttest and on interviews dealing with the approach and the use of advanced strategies for number facts.

• Wood, T. and P. Sellers. 1997. "Deepening the Analysis: Longitudinal Assessment of a Problem-Centered Mathematics Program." *Journal of Research in Mathematics Education*, 28 (2): 163–186.

This evaluation study of the Purdue Problem-Centered Mathematics Project is one of several over the past few years. In this report, the primary comparison is of students who had been in the project for both second and third grade and those who had received textbook instruction both years. The results indicated that the former students had significantly higher standardized mathematics achievement (including computation), better conceptual understanding, and more task-oriented beliefs for learning than the textbook group. These differences remained the following year when both groups received textbook instruction.

References

Articles and Reports

Bebout, H. C. and T. P. Carpenter. 1989. "Assessing and Building Thinking Strategies: Necessary Bases for Instruction." In *New Directions for Elementary School Mathematics, 1989 Yearbook*, ed. P. Trafton, 59–69. Reston, VA: National Council of Teachers of Mathematics.

Campbell, P. F. 1997. "Connecting Instructional Practice to Student Thinking." *Teaching Children Mathematics*, 4 (2): 106–110.

Carpenter, T. P., D. A. Carey, and V. L. Kouba. 1990. "A Problem-Solving Approach to the Operations." In *Mathematics for the Young Child*, ed. J. N. Payne, 111–132. Reston, VA: National Council of Teachers of Mathematics.

Howden, H. 1989. "Teaching Number Sense." *Arithmetic Teacher*, 36 (6): 6–11.

Lester, J. B. 1996. "Establishing a Community of Mathematics Learners." In *What's Happening in Math Class? Envisioning New Practices Through Teacher Narratives*, ed. D. Schifter, 88–102. New York: Teachers College Press.

National Council of Teachers of Mathematics. 1991. *Professional Standards for Teaching Mathematics*. Reston, VA: National Council of Teachers of Mathematics.

———. 1989. *Curriculum and Evaluation Standards for School Mathematics*. Reston, VA: National Council of Teachers of Mathematics.

National Research Council. 1989. *Everybody Counts: A Report to the Nation On the Future of Mathematical Education*. Washington, D.C.: National Academy Press.

Resnick, L. B.. 1995. "Inventing Arithmetic: Making Children's Intuition Work in School." In *Basic and Applied Perspectives on Learning, Cognition, and Development*, ed. C. A. Nelson, 75–101. Hillsdale, NJ: Erlbaum.

Resnick, L. B., V. L. Bill, S. B. Lesgold, and M. N. Leer. 1991. "Thinking in Arithmetic Class." In *Teaching Advanced Skills to At-Risk Students: Views from Research and Practice*, ed. B. Means, C. Chelemer, and M. S. Knapp, 27–53. San Francisco: Jossey-Bass.

Trafton, P. and C. Hartman. 1988. "Developing Number Sense and Computational Strategies in Problem-Centered classrooms." *Teaching Children Mathematics,* 4 (4) 230–233.

Teaching/Curriculum Resources

Burns, M. 1992. *Math and Literature: Book 1 (K–3).* Sausalito, CA: Math Solutions Publications.

Burns, M. 1994. *Math by All Means: Place Value, Grade 2.* Sausalito, CA: Math Solutions Publications.

Burns, M. and B. Tank. 1988. *A Collection of Math Lessons: From Grades 1 Through 3.* Sausalito, CA: Math Solutions Publications.

Robertson, L., et al. 1999. *Number Power: A Cooperative Approach to Mathematics and Social Development.* 9 Volumes, K–6. Oakland, CA: Developmental Studies Center.

Russell, S. J., K. Economopoulos, M. Murray, J. Mokros, A. Goodrow. 1997. *Investigations in Number, Data, and Space, Grade 1 and Grade 2.* Palo Alto, CA: Dale Seymour Publications.

Russell, S. J. and A. Stone. 1990. *Counting: Ourselves and Our Families from Used Numbers: Real Data in the Classroom.* Palo Alto, CA: Dale Seymour Publications.

Scales, D. 1986. *Our Second Big Book of Numbers.* Crystal Lake, IL: Rigby.

Thiessen, D., M. Matthias, and J. Smith. 1998. *The Wonderful World of Mathematics: A Critically Annotated List of Children's Books in Mathematics.* Reston, VA: National Council of Teachers of Mathematics.

University of Illinois at Chicago. 1997. *Math Trailblazers: A Mathematical Journey Using Science and Language Arts (A TIMS Curriculum).* Dubuque, IA: Kendall/Hunt.

Whitin, D. J. and S. Wilde. 1991. *Read Any Good Math Lately?: Children's Books for Mathematical Learning,* K–6. Portsmouth, NH: Heinemann.

Children's Books

Axelrod, A. 1994. *Pigs Will Be Pigs.* Illustrated by S. McGinley-Nally. New York: Simon & Schuster.

Carle, E. 1971. *Rooster's Off to the See the World.* Natick, MA: Picture Book Studio.

Clement, R. 1991. *Counting on Frank.* Milwaukee, WI: Gareth Stevens Children's Books.

Crews, D. 1986. *Ten Black Dots.* New York: Greenwillow.

Emberley, E. 1984. *Ed Emberley's Picture Pie: A Circle Drawing Book.* Boston: Little, Brown.

Hutchins, P. 1986. *The Doorbell Rang.* New York: Greenwillow Books.

Kirk, D. 1994. *Miss Spider's Tea Party.* Illustrated by A. White. New York: Scholastic.

Mahy, M. 1987. *17 Kings and 42 Elephants.* Pictures by P. MacCarthy. New York: Dial.

Merriam, E. 1993. *Twelve Ways to Get Eleven.* Illustrated by B. Karlin. New York: Simon & Schuster.

Pinczes, E. J. 1991. *One Hundred Hungry Ants.* Illustrated by B. MacKain. Boston: Houghton Mifflin.

Scieszka, J. 1995. *Math Curse.* Illustrated by L. Smith. New York: Viking.

Viorst, J. 1993. *Alexander Who Used to Be Rich Last Sunday.* Illustrated by Ray Cruz. New York: Atheneum.

White, E. B. 1952. *Charlotte's Web.* Illustrations by G. Williams. New York: HarperCollins.